Know Bristol

To Anjali

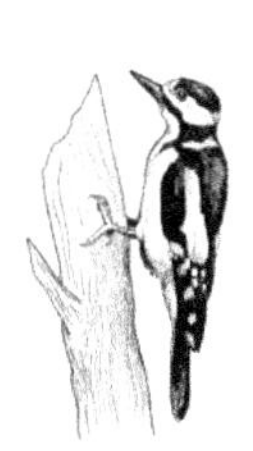

Great Spotted Books

ISBN No. 978-1-914512-05-6

Cover illustration by Pradipta Mukherjee

Know Bristol

Returning to Bristol a few years ago I set out to rediscover the city I had grown up in during the 90s and early 2000s. A self-proclaimed "tourist in my own city", I was amazed to find that, even as someone who has actively researched the city's past for many years, there was still a lot I did not know.

I soon found myself blurting my little nuggets of information at my family and friends who, until now, have borne the brunt of a lifelong enthusiasm for the city. Eventually, I stopped blurting at my friends and starting blurting onto paper, the result of which is this book.

Know Bristol is 365 nuggets of largely historical information which will hopefully be of interest to anyone keen to learn a bit more about where they live.

If you do read this book at the rate of one fact per day, you should find a few key dates in the city's history will line up as you go along.

Know Bristol roams across maritime, industrial, social, military, political, royal and cultural history, picking out key events and people or sometimes just quirky information.

If I was to identify one single motivation for putting this together it is simply to contribute to our collective sense of place.

I often find that people who profess not to be particularly interested in history turn out to be very interested in the history of where they live. How could you not be interested in the story behind the streets you walk every day, or the church you attend, or the shops you visit?

There is a very tangible quality to local history which can help reintroduce people to subject matter they have been disengaged from, either through bad teaching or an education system focused on dates and the churning out of essays written for the convenience of the people marking them.

One drawback of local history is the propensity to exaggerate or over-simplify. An individual who *may* have invented one *aspect* of a particular product and at one time lived in the city but *years before he or she did that* soon becomes "the inventor of Tarmac lived in Bristol". It has been amazing to see how many variations of the truth exist in the city, and not always easy to work out which version is the most reliable. I've been careful to add appropriate qualifications to much of the information laid out here – so there is a lot of "we understand that.." or "it is believed to be..." which may not make for thrilling reading but it does at least show where there are some questions still unanswered.

Finally, as you dip in and out of Know Bristol, I hope this book will inspire you to find out a bit more, and hopefully you will become a tourist of your own city too.

It is strange that many of us travel hundreds of miles on European excursions, returning to the UK with bucketloads of information about European cities but won't extend that enthusiasm for knowledge to the city we actually live in. I suspect there are many people in the city who have visited the great churches of France or Spain but never even set foot in St Mary Redcliffe. Next time you are looking for a weekend getaway, consider taking yourself to the less-explored parts of Bristol, it might be just the break you need.

Acknowledgements

Know Bristol is dedicated to my aunt, who although not a Bristolian, recently celebrated her

60th birthday and has always supported my writing projects. Thank you also to Nina Sofia (editor) and Pradipta Mukherjee (illustrator), and my parents for housing me during the creation of this book.

I want to acknowledge the many Bristol enthusiasts, local historians, and institutions who have made much of the information in this book available to the wider public and who have helped, directly or indirectly, with the research for this book.

About Bristol, Aerospace Bristol, Avon Wildlife Trust, Barton Hill History Group, Bristol Archives, Bristol and Avon Archaeological Society, Bristol City Council, BristolCityDocks.co.uk, Bristol City Museum & Galleries, Bristol Cable, BristolFloatingHarbour.co.uk, Bristol Industrial Archaeology Society, Bristol Radical History Group, Bristol Post, Bristol 24/7, The Bristol

Magazine, Bristol Tree Forum, Bristol Zoological Society, Christopher Baker, Anton Bantock MBE, John Bartlett, Eugene Byrne, Tom Brothwell, Centre for the Study of the Legacies of British Slavery (UCL), Clifton Suspension Bridge Trust, Design West, English Heritage, Friends of the Avon Gorge and Downs, Friends of Troopers Hill, Historic England, Graeme Churchard, Rosemary Clinch, Madge Dresser, Jane Duffus, Kingsley Fulbrook, Imperial War Museum, Mike Jenner, Andy King, Neil Maggs, Michael Manson, National Historic Ships UK, National Trust, Catherine Pitt, OutStories Bristol, Dagmar Smeed, Charlie Revell-Smith, Andrew Swift, Elizabeth Ralph, Rhian Rowson, Severn Estuary Partnership, SS Great Britain Trust, University of Bristol, UWE, Visit Bristol.

1

Bristol has been called *Brycgstow, Brigstow and Brigg Stow*

Bristol's name is thought to be derived from Old English meaning "the place by the bridge" or "meeting place by the bridge". The earliest written record of the town, from 1051, has it as "Brycgstow". Its spelling changed several times and is thought to refer to a bridge in the vicinity of what is now Bristol Bridge. However, it could be attributed to a few different bridges which existed in the 11th century when the early settlement is believed to have been established. There have been some suggestions that the "Terminal L" added to the name is a result of the Bristolian accent.

2

The chains of the Clifton Suspension Bridge once hung over the Thames

Although work on the bridge began in 1831, it wasn't finished until 1864, four years after Brunel's death. In the intervening time, the project ran out of money and the final design differed from Brunel's original, including a greatly strengthened and widened roadway. The chains that were used to support the Clifton Suspension Bridge were recovered from Brunel's Hungerford Bridge. Built as a footbridge to draw Londoners to Hungerford Market, it was demolished in 1863. Two masonry piers survived and now support the Golden Jubilee Bridge.

3

The largest WWII bomb dropped on Bristol failed to explode

As many as 10 percent of the bombs dropped on Bristol failed to explode and some are thought to still be under the city and the surrounding area. Between the 3rd and 4th of January 1941, Bristol suffered the longest single raid of the Bristol Blitz. Over the course of 12 hours, 149 people lost their lives. One of the bombs dropped was the largest design in use by the Luftwaffe at the time. Nicknamed "Satan", the 4,000lb (1,800kg) bomb landed on Beckington Road, Knowle, but failed to explode. It was recovered in 1943 and later paraded in London during VE Day celebrations.

4

Bristol has 13 lost railway stations

War damaged, saddled with debt, and struggling to compete with road transport, Britain's nationalised railway network was desperately in need of reform during the 1950s. The Macmillan government put Dr Richard Beeching in charge of a comprehensive review of Britain's railway network focused on massive efficiency savings. In the notorious "Beeching cuts" that followed, around a third of Britain's rail network, roughly 5,000 miles, was torn up along with 2,363 stations. Not all of Bristol's lost stations were put out of use by Beeching, but the ones that were included: Henbury, Ashley Hill, Clifton Bridge, Chittening Platform, Fishponds, Horfield, and St Anne's Park.

5

Bristol Cathedral was an Augustinian Abbey

The abbey was founded in 1140 by Robert Fitzharding (later Lord Berkeley). The abbey and the monastic order of St Augustine was the largest and best funded of monastic houses that existed at the time and is the namesake for Canon's Marsh, St Augustine's Parade, St Augustine's Reach, Abbots Leigh and Abbots Pool. The pool, which still exists today, was part of an out-of-town retreat for the monks and seized along with most of Abbots Leigh and Leigh Woods at the time of the dissolution of the monasteries in 1539. The Abbey Gatehouse, Chapter House and Elder Lady Chapel are amongst the most impressive abbey-era features still present at the cathedral site today.

6

The BBC Symphony Orchestra was moved to Bristol during WWII

The orchestra's founder, conductor Sir Adrian Boult CH was moved to a house in Leigh Woods, while the orchestra was based at Pembroke Road. Heavy bombing during the war, including a raid that killed a bass player and his wife, meant the orchestra was moved again, this time to Bedfordshire. It was whilst conducting at Colston Hall that Boult found out his flat in London was destroyed in a raid, including his own personal recordings. Boult would go on to conduct the music at the coronation of Queen Elizabeth II and has a memorial stone in Westminster Abbey.

7

Eugénie de Montijo, Empress of the French, went to school in Clifton

Eugénie and her sister Paca attended a school at No.2, Royal York Crescent in 1837, but found it not to their taste. Paca told her mother Clifton was boring, and Eugénie attempted to escape to India, getting as far as boarding a boat in Bristol City Docks with two equally disgruntled Indian pupils of the school before being tracked down by her teachers. Napoleon III, the nephew of Napoleon I, became Emperor of the French in 1852 following a term as president 1848-1852. After a period of resisting his advances, he married Eugénie on 30th January 1853, two weeks after their engagement.

8

Every British Concorde had its maiden flight from here

Concorde was a supersonic passenger-carrying aircraft that could fly at twice the speed of sound. Developed in an Anglo-French partnership, the airliner had its wings and engines developed at Filton. Although the original aim was to produce Concordes for the wider aviation industry, in the end only 20 were ever made. Ten of these were produced at Filton, the other ten in Toulouse, France. Today you can see a complete Concorde (British Airways Concorde 216 (G-BOAF)) at the Bristol Aerospace Museum. Better known as Alpha Foxtrot, it was both the last Concorde to be built and the last to fly.

9

Bristol used to have its own time zone

Until the opening of the Great Western Railway in 1838, Bristol was 11 minutes behind Greenwich Mean Time. In a sense this is "true" Bristol time or "solar time", based on Bristol's position relative to the sun and 2º 35' (West) of Greenwich. The advent of railway timetables meant times had to be standardised across the country. Bristol tried to cling on to its own time zone after the construction of the GWR but was eventually forced to change, along with the rest of the country, as the railway network continued to spread. Conformity to GMT became law in 1880 but the clock on the Corn Exchange building still has two-minute hands, a red one for GMT and a black one for Bristol Time.

10

Temple Church tower is leaning over by 2.7 degrees

Best known as Bristol's "very own Leaning Tower of Pisa", the church does not quite match Pisa's 3.97-degree tilt. The lean is understood to be caused by the weight of the tower on the soft clay foundations of the church and means that the top of Temple's tower is fully 1.6 metres out of kilter with the base. The original 12th century church was built for the Knights Templar, a round prominent medieval military order, and it is thought to have been their South West headquarters. Construction of the famous tower began in the 1390s but was halted due to the lean, and building work did not begin again until 1460. The tower survived the Bristol Blitz, sadly the rest of the church did not.

11

An underground railway runs from Clifton to Hotwells

The entrance to the "Clifton Rocks Railway" is located next to the Avon Gorge Hotel where you can clearly see tracks running towards Hotwells from the roadside. The line opened as a water-powered funicular railway in 1893, providing a route down to a station by the river, the remains of which are still visible from Portway. The railway failed to attract passenger numbers and closed in 1934, but the tunnel had a useful purpose during WWII as a bomb-proof relay station for sending secure government messages, an air raid shelter for local residents, and as an emergency studio for the BBC.

12

In *Treasure Island*, the *Hispaniola* sails from Bristol

Squire Trelawney finds the ship in Bristol and finds the crew courtesy of Long John Silver, who owns a pub on the docks called "The Spyglass". Long John is married to a woman of African descent who helps manage his business interests. Trelawney stays at a fictional Bristolian "Old Anchor Inn" and writes to Doctor Livesey from there. "The Admiral Benbow" is another fictional inn, located outside Bristol in the book and supposedly inspired by the Llandoger Trow on Kings Street. The Bristol-born pirate known as Blackbeard had a second in command called Israel Hands, subsequently the name given to the *Hispaniola's* mutinous coxswain.

13

Henry Cruger is the only person to have served in both the UK Parliament and the New York State Senate

Henry Cruger succeeded in becoming a common councilman for Bristol (1766-90), then Sheriff of the city (1766-7) and Mayor (1781-2). In the meantime, Cruger was appointed as a warden, and later Master of the Society of Merchant Venturers (1781). He served two terms as MP for Bristol and then returned to the US and took up a seat as a New York State Senator (1792–1796). He lived on Great George Street and was connected with slavery through his business interests in the trade with West India.

14

A bell from a Royal Naval aircraft carrier is used to announce the start of services in Bristol Cathedral

Originally under construction as an ocean liner named *Conte Rosso* the 172-metre-long HMS Argus is considered to be the first working example of modern aircraft carrier design. The vessel was commissioned for use during WWI but would not see action until WWII. The ship's bell found its way to the cathedral after the ship was scrapped in 1946. It can be found at the South Transept near the entrance to the East Cloister and is rung at the start of significant services.

15

Bristol has its very own Byzantine Empire-inspired architectural style

Popular in the late Victorian period and unique to Bristol, surviving buildings built in the "Bristol Byzantine Revival Style" include the Old Carriage Works in Stokes Croft, the Old Soap Factory (latterly Gardiner Haskins, Christopher Thomas Court and the Soapworks apartments), the Granary on Welsh Back, Robinson's Warehouse in Bathurst Basin, the Arnolfini, and the Bristol Beacon. Though often intended for industrial use, many of these buildings now rank amongst the most distinctive historic buildings in the city and several have protected listed status.

16

Sea Mills predates Bristol

Now engulfed by a much-expanded City of Bristol, Sea Mills can trace its roots back to the Ancient Roman, predating the true founding of Bristol by almost 1,000 years. The Romans established a port settlement known as Portus Abonae at (what is now) Sea Mills on the banks of the River Avon in the year 1AD. Between 1AD and 4AD the site is believed to have been a military town and fort that was once connected to Bath by road. What little survives of Abonae is now considered by Historic England to be "very rare in the national context" due to the comparatively early settlement. The town appears to have been abandoned and was not resettled by the Saxons.

17

An annual celebration encourages fruit trees to provide a bountiful harvest

While most wassailing celebrations now take place on 5th January, a few recognise "Old Twelvy", the date before the introduction of the Gregorian calendar in 1752, now 17th January. In a tradition maintained in some parts of Bristol and Somerset, fruit trees are blessed and songs are sung including this extract from an 1871 wassail:

Here's to thee, old apple tree,
Whence thou mayst bud
And whence thou mayst blow!
And whence thou mayst bear apples enow!

18

One of Hollywood’s greatest “leading men” was born in Horfield

Perhaps the best-known actor of his generation, Cary Grant was born Archibald Alexander Leach on 18th January 1904 at 15 Hughenden Road, Horfield. His enthusiasm for the entertainment business was nurtured at the Bristol Hippodrome where he worked as a junior stagehand, a position colloquially known as a “goefer”. He grew up in a poor household and had an alcoholic father and a mother who had, unknown to the young Grant, been sectioned at the Bristol Insane Asylum. He died in 1986 but consistently tops polls of the world’s greatest actors decades later.

19

Daniel Day-Lewis trained at the Old Vic Theatre School

The three-time Oscar winner is one of several famous faces that learnt their trade in Bristol. Naomi Harris, Olivia Colman CBE, Gene Wilder, Jeremy Irons, Maisie Williams, Sir Patrick Stewart, Miranda Richardson, Annette Crosibie and Patricia Routledge are just a few others. Bristol also has an unusual number of comedy connections. Sir Bob Hope, Stephen Merchant, Lee Evans, Russell Howard and Kerry Howard were all born in Bristol. David Walliams OBE, Matt Lucas and Marcus Brigstocke studied Drama at the University of Bristol, whilst Simon Pegg holds a BA in Film, Theatre and Television from the university. John Cleese was educated at Clifton College.

20

The US state of Pennsylvania is named after a Bristolian

Admiral Sir William Penn was born in Bristol on 23rd April 1621. He was christened in the Church of St Thomas the Martyr and went on to become MP for Weymouth and a successful naval officer. His son, also William Penn, was given the land which became the Province of Pennsylvania by King Charles II to settle debts owed by the Crown to his father. The junior Penn named the new province after his father. The church where elder the Penn was christened has survived and is now open to visitors free-of-charge. He was buried at St Mary Redcliffe and a memorial to him is on display inside the church.

21

The sewage treatment works at Avonmouth handles over 200 million litres of sewage every day

The enormous site processes wastewater from Bristol's four main sewage outlets. Prior to its construction in the 1960s, untreated wastewater flowed out into Severn Estuary. Now operated by Wessex Water, the treatment works are occasionally opened to visitors. In 2020, one of the worst industrial tragedies in Bristol's recent history took place at the site when a silo containing biosolids exploded, killing three employees and one contractor and injuring another.

22

Ships built in Bristol served in the East India Company

In an extreme example of capitalism-gone-wrong, the British East India Company rose to become the dominant commercial and military power on the Indian subcontinent during the 1700s. "Company rule" of India continued up until the start of the Raj in 1858. The firm operated a brutal and highly extractive regime and was widely blamed for a famine in 1770 in which as many as ten million people are estimated to have died. Based in London, very little Company trade made its way to Bristol but several Company ships, known as East Indiamen, were built in Bristol including *Enchantress* (1828), *Fame* (1801), *Kingston* (1811), *Lady Carrington* (1809), *Henry Porcher* (1817), *Woodford* (1829), and *Waterloo* (1815).

23

Wallace & Gromit is made in Bristol

Aardman Animations Ltd, the producers of *Chicken Run*, *Morph* and *Creature Comforts*, are based near the SS Great Britain on Gas Ferry Road. The company was founded on 12th April 1972 by Peter Lord and David Sproxton. *Wallace and Gromit* is the brainchild of multi-Academy Award and BAFTA winning creator Nick Park CBE, but its aesthetic is influenced more by Park's hometown of Preston than Bristol. *Chicken Run*, produced by Aardman and directed by Park in 2000, quickly became the highest grossing stop motion animated feature film of all time.

24

Bristol institutions campaigned to keep Bristol in the slave trade

Part of a much broader "West India Interest", both the forerunner to Bristol City Council (the Corporation), and the Society of Merchant Venturers lobbied the Crown and Parliament for the protection of the slave trade. The Merchant Venturers, which has its origins in a 13th century guild and survives as a charitable organisation, successfully petitioned against Wilberforce's first attempt to get the slave trade abolished in Parliament. These organisations, backed by the city's MPs, were successful in delaying both the abolition of slavery and the slave trade.

25

Brunel's first ship, the *Great Western*, was constructed at Wapping Wharf

Launched on 19th July 1837, at 71 metres long, the *SS Great Western* was the largest ship in the world and the fastest way to get to New York at the time. She was an engineering marvel of her time, and the very first purpose-built steamship made for transatlantic voyages. Allegedly conceived during a board meeting of the Great Western Railway, Brunel regarded a steamship connection to New York as the logical next step for his pioneering Bristol to London line. Like the *SS Great Britain*, she was later used as a troopship in the Crimean War of 1856 before being broken up for scrap.

26

The first modern hot air balloon was designed and built in Bristol

Don Cameron moved to Bristol in the 60s and, along with other members of the Bristol Gliding Club, is responsible for the creation of the Bristol Belle in 1967. He founded Cameron Balloons in Cotham in 1971 and the company soon became the largest manufacturer of hot air balloons worldwide. The Bristol International Balloon Fiesta started in 1979 and is Europe's largest annual meeting of hot air balloons. Air Balloon Hill and Air Balloon Road (St George) get their names from much earlier balloon exploits; specifically, an unmanned flight that landed on the hill in 1784.

27

The first steam engine used for non-industrial purposes was used in the grounds of Goldney Hall

A tower in the grounds of Goldney Hall (Clifton Wood) was constructed in 1764 to house a steam engine which pumped water into the garden's fountain and grotto. Today the hall, formerly a private home, is used as student accommodation by the University of Bristol but the impressive tower still stands and is just about visible from outside the wall. The grounds, which boast an orchard, orangery, rotunda and an 18th century grotto are occasionally open to visitors.

28

Both James May and "The Stig" were born in Bristol

British racing driver Ben Collins was born in Bristol and had a successful career in motorsport before his stint as The Stig on BBC's popular *Top Gear* motoring programme. May was also born in Bristol but spent most of his childhood elsewhere. Chris Harris, another *Top Gear* presenter and racing car driver, lived just outside Bristol and attended Clifton College. May only spent a year in Bristol but in 2013 he told reporters that the West Country feels like home and he "thinks" his parents got engaged at Weston-Super-Mare. During his time as a presenter on the programme, *Top Gear* became the BBC's most widely watched and commercially successful TV series.

29

Bristol Zoo Gardens is the fifth oldest zoo in the world

The Bristol Zoological Society was founded 22nd July 1835 and included Isambard Kingdom Brunel among the original shareholders. The Clifton site opened to the public on 11th July 1836, making it the oldest zoo in the world outside of a capital city. Over the years the zoo became home to elephants, tigers, giraffes and polar bears. Although many of the first animals and their enclosures would not be considered appropriate today, the zoo became a very popular attraction and later evolved into a centre of conservation, pioneering the protection of endangered species. A detailed account can be found in Dr Andy Flack's *The Wild Within: Histories of a Landmark British Zoo.*

30

Around 2,000 people drowned in the Bristol Channel flood of 1607

On 30th January 1607, a storm surge made its way up the Bristol Channel, flooding 200 miles of the English countryside. The pace of the surge, "faster than a greyhound could run", according to contemporary accounts, meant people did not have time to escape. Bristol was protected from the worst ravages of the surge but did experience a rise in the height of the River Avon. In the Old City, the floodwater was high enough to cover a man. It took ten days for the water to recede, by which time a theory that the flood was a warning from God had become the dominant explanation.

31

Bristol tried to stay neutral in the English Civil War

The city's merchants and administrators petitioned both the King and the Parliamentarians to find a peaceful settlement and leave Bristol out of the First English Civil War which ran from 1642 to 1651. Bristol was an important city for both sides in the war, but it had long been controlled by mercantile interests who largely favoured good business conditions over ideological battles. The city's merchants would later petition for peace with the American colonies at the start of the American War of Independence for much the same reason. Bristol fell to the Parliamentarians (1642), then to the Royalists (1643) and again to the Parliamentarians (1645).

32

Megan Markle officially opened the new Bristol Old Vic Theatre foyer in 2019

Crowds of onlookers gathered in the snow to see the Duke and Duchess of Sussex visiting Bristol on 1st February 2019. Then still working members of the royal family, the couple also visited Empire Fighting Chance, a charity in Easton that supports young people through boxing and fitness, as well as the St Pauls based women's charity One25. At Empire Fighting Chance, Prince Harry spoke to a teenager who had recently suffered bereavement about his own experiences of losing his mother. Megan helped to prepare bags of food and clothing for the female sex workers helped by One25.

33

Albert II took part in an exchange programme here

Albert Alexandre Louis Pierre Grimaldi (Prince Albert) became the ruler of Monaco, the sovereign city-state on the south coast of France in 2005. The young prince attended the University of Bristol's Alfred Marshall School of Economics and Management in 1979. He is not the university's only royal connection; David Mohato Bereng Seeiso, later King of Lesotho, (Lestie III) studied a diploma in English law at Bristol in the 80s. Several politicians have also graduated from the university including Theresa Villiers, Stephen Crabb and the second Prime Minister of Belize, Sir Manuel Esquivel, who was a postgraduate in Physics at the university.

34

St Werburgh is the patron saint of Chester

We might associate the saint with east Bristol but her patronage went to the town of Chester in the county of Cheshire. The St Werburgh district of Bristol is named after St Werburgh's Church, which in turn is named after the 8th century Anglo Saxon princess. The church was originally located at Corn Street where it adjoined the Commercial Rooms and is believed to have been the site of a place of worship dating back to Saxon times. Road widening in the early 1870s necessitated the church being moved, along with 40 chests of human remains and around 100 lead coffins. The bodies were re-interred at Greenbank Cemetery (Easton) and, much later, the church was used as a climbing centre.

35

Ribena was invented here

Keen to utilise the naturally high levels of vitamin C found in blackcurrants, Dr Vernon Charley developed the original syrup at Bristol University's Long Ashton Research Station (LARS) in 1933. It was subsequently produced commercially by HW Carter & Co and a factory was established on North Street, Bedminster in 1936. With fruit supplies restricted during WWII, Ribena was handed out to children for free and would become one of the country's most popular soft drinks brands. The factory was moved to Coleford, Gloucestershire, in 1947. Originally set up in the late 1800s to study the production of cider, LARS continued to make important contributions to agricultural science up until its closure in 2003.

36

Elizabeth Blackwell was the first woman to receive a medical degree in the US

Born in Bristol in February 1821, Blackwell is better remembered in America than in her hometown. Her determination to train as a physician was set against a backdrop of extraordinary prejudice from both the public and the medical establishment. She received a medical degree from Geneva Medical College in New York in 1849, having been admitted "as a joke" by the all-male student body two years earlier. Blackwell also became the first woman on the British General Medical Council Register. In 1974 she appeared on the American 18 cent stamp.

37

Churchill and Thatcher were both honorary members of the Society of Merchant Venturers

A portrait of Churchill by Arthur Pan hangs in Merchants' Hall and the dining room features a large war-damaged coat of arms from the original Merchants' Hall in the Old City. The building was destroyed during the Bristol Blitz in 1940 and it was Churchill's idea to re-hang the coat of arms as a reminder of the destruction brought about by the aerial bombing of Bristol. The Merchants were temporarily relocated to what was Fern House on The Promenade in Clifton Down in 1945. They later combined Fern and Auckland houses to create the new hall.

38

Bristol is the only city other than London that has a State Coach

Constructed by Fullers in the 1860s, the State Coach was built to transport the Lord Mayor of Bristol on civic occasions. The City also has a Landau carriage, which is used on Rush Sunday and Remembrance, and a more modern vehicle known as the Proclamation Brake, which is housed at the M Shed museum and became part of the council's fleet after WWII. A bizarre looking vehicle, it was developed by Sir George White, subsequently acquired by the Council and named after the practice of proclaiming the crowning of a new sovereign to the city from the Lord Mayor's carriage.

39

Over 500,000 enslaved Africans were transported to on Bristol-owned vessels

90 per cent of British involvement in the transatlantic slave trade was conducted out of just three port cities in the UK. Liverpool-based academic Anthony Tibbles estimates 5,300 voyages took place from Liverpool, 3,100 left from London, and Bristol ships took part in 2,200 voyages. The profits from slavery were instrumental in launching Britain as the world's preeminent power and while the conditions of slavery are hard to imagine, much of Bristol's surviving historic environment has links to this dark period in the city's history.

40

Solitary bees thrive at Troopers Hill

Troopers Hill has been famous for many things over the years, particularly the production of brass and copper and its connections with the English Civil War. The Council acquired 21 acres of land here in 1956 and the site became a nature reserve. The protection of the hill has created a degree of residential security for some of the West Country's most important pollinators. We tend to think of bees as living in hives but as the name suggests, solitary bees live independent lives and make their nests in the ground or in wood or stone cavities.
Troopers Hill is a locally important site for these bees with 83 different bee species recorded there in the years up to 2021.

41

Seven ships have born the name “HMS Bristol”

The first of these ships was fitted with 48 guns, went into service in 1653, and was later captured by the French. A subsequent vessel, a 50-gun ship launched in 1775, served in the American War of Independence. Two recent HMS Bristols saw action off the Falkland Islands: in 1914 against the Imperial German Navy, and in 1982 when the HMS Bristol served as flagship. Decommissioned in 2020 following a stint as a training ship, D23 was the only vessel of its kind, the other Type 82 destroyers having been cancelled following the 1966 Strategic Defence Review. Council House and the Lord Mayor’s official residence at Mansion House all feature paintings of HMS Bristols.

42

The River Frome runs under the City Centre

Back when Bristol principally existed within its medieval walls (what we now call "the Old City"), the Frome would have partially encircled the city. The first major diversion of the Frome is thought to have begun in 1240 with the digging out of what is now called St Augustine's Reach. This took seven years to complete and was undertaken to improve the docking space for Bristol's busy port. The Frome was gradually covered over (culverted) between 1860 and 1890 but still flows out from under the City Centre into St Augustine's Reach and can be partially navigated by boat.

43

The last ship to be built here was the *Miranda Guinness*

The world's first liquid bulk carrier commissioned for the transportation of beer, the *MV Miranda Guinness*, was built in Albion dock by Charles Hill & Sons in 1976. The ship was named after the wife of the then chairman of Guinness, Miranda Daphne Jane Guinness, Countess of Iveagh. *MV Miranda Guinness* joined the Guinness fleet in 1977, transporting up to 6,500 barrels (two million pints) per voyage between Liverpool and Dublin. The *Miranda* made headlines when she hit Dublin's East-Link Bridge in 1985. She was scrapped along with the only remaining Guinness ship (*Patricia*) in 1993 as the company moved to transportable tanks.

44

Vale Street is the steepest street in England

With an incline of 22-degrees, Vale Street is steep even by Bristol's standards. The Ordnance Survey has declared it England's steepest street and fully five degrees steeper than the next steepest street, Old Wyche Road, in Worcestershire. Residents have to tie their cars to lampposts in icy weather to stop them sliding down the hill and many take part in the street's annual Easter egg rolling competition. In December 2020, a Banksy mural depicting a woman sneezing out her false teeth appeared on the side of a house on Vale Street, temporarily making the road a destination for street art enthusiasts across the country. The Banksy was subsequently sold off.

45

A system of man-made caves runs underneath Redcliffe

The caves are thought to weave under about an acre of land and are the result of centuries of mining for Redcliffe Sandstone, a Triassic rock which serviced the glassmaking and pottery trade. Despite being widely known as the Redcliffe Caves, these are really a system of entirely manmade mine excavations. A long-held rumour that the caves were created to house slaves is almost certainly untrue but there is evidence to support the idea that prisoners from the Napoleonic Wars were held there. During WWII a large bomb resulted in the caving-in of most of the Redcliffe Caves. No map exists of the full cave system, which may extend for as much as 12 acres under Redcliffe.

46

A dinosaur was found on Durdham Down

The Downs were heavily quarried in Victorian times, mostly for limestone, and many of these quarry sites can still be seen today. Often called the "Bristol Dinosaur", Thecodontosaurus was discovered in a limestone quarry bordering on Clifton in 1834, before any dinosaurs had been formally recognised. It was not until 1843 that it was given its name, which means "socket toothed lizard". The two-legged dinosaur is around 210 million years old and was the first dinosaur discovered from the Triassic (251 to 201 million years ago) and the fourth described by science. This makes it a very early dinosaur, living 49 million years before Diplodocus and 145 million years before Tyrannosaurus.

47

Castle Park had a castle

Constructed in 1088, Bristol Castle was once one of the largest royal fortresses in England and featured in many of the most important political dramas during the medieval period. Over the years high-profile prisoners, such as Eleanor of Brittany, Stephen of Blois and the last princes of Gwynedd, would find themselves confined within the castle walls. Oliver Cromwell had the castle demolished in 1656 and what little remains today includes part of the moat, a small tunnel, a sally port and vaulted chambers that may once have led to the great hall. Perhaps the most prominent reminder of the castle is its depiction in the city's coat of arms, which shows a ship leaving the castle's Water Gate, a variation of which is used as the logo for Bristol City Council.

48

In the 2000s, around 750,000 vehicles were imported into the Port of Bristol every year

Of the port's 2,600-acre estate, 500 acres were set aside as compounds for cars imported into the UK and have been clearly visible from Avonmouth Bridge. Previously owned by the council, the port which includes both Royal Portbury and Avonmouth Docks was privatised in 1991. According to the company that took over the port, the Bristol Port Company, in 2020 the docks were responsible for 27 per cent of all UK aviation fuel imports, 25 per cent of all animal feed imports and ten per cent of UK coal imports for electricity generation.

49

Kingswood was "the king's wood"

The forest of Kingswood once covered around 18 square miles and extended as far as the River Severn. It was a royal hunting ground for Saxon and then Norman royalty, and would have encompassed Pucklechurch "palace", believed to be the site of King Edmund I's murder in 946. The forest was gradually cleared to make way for farmland while the wood was used for fuel and building material. Another industry that drove the conversion of Kingswood from forest to human use was the area's productive coal seams. By 1675, around 500 packhorses were employed in the transportation of coal to Bristol and the area continued to be one of the principal sources of coal to the city in the 1700s and 1800s.

50

The first American embassy in Britain was in Bristol

Having argued against conflict with the Americans, Bristol's merchants went on to defy instructions from London and made a request for a representative from the newly formed United States of America. In 1792, Elias Vanderhorst was appointed as consul to the Port of Bristol and the surrounding area by President Washington and Secretary of State, Thomas Jefferson. He set up shop at No.37, Queen's Square. The Bristol Archives holds a copy of the letter confirming his appointment signed by both Washington and Jefferson. The archives also hold Elias' diary in which he states that the social life of Bristol was so vibrant he struggled to find the time to work.

51

Bristol is a widely used namesake

There are 35 populated Bristols around the world, most of which are in the United States, but there are also two populated Bristols in Canada, and one in Barbados, Peru, Costa Rica and Jamaica respectively. Of these Bristols, Connecticut's boasts the second largest population of "Bristolians" outside of the UK's Bristol with over 61,000 inhabitants. Pennsylvania's Bristol has the third largest population and the distinction of being part of a state that is itself named after a Bristolian (Sir William Penn). Outside of the States, Canada's Florenceville-Bristol is home to McCain Foods, the world's largest producer of French fries and frozen potato products.

52

There are three known Iron Age Hillforts within Bristol

The three hill forts at Clifton Down (Observatory Hill), Kings Weston and Blaise Castle were in use during the Iron Age (550BC – 1AD). These sites pre-date Bristol by more than a thousand years and very little is known about what the area may have been like at the time. Evidence has been found of dwellings around the River Avon which would have been occupied in the summer and then abandoned during flooding in the winter. It has been speculated that the Avon may have been a boundary between the Clifton Down camp and the camps of Stokeleigh and Burwalls in Leigh Woods.

53

The third Earl of Bristol is the namesake for Bristol Bay

The third Earl of Bristol was Augustus Hervey (1724-1799), the namesake of Bristol Bay (Alaska), Bristol Island (South Sandwich Islands) and by extension the Bristol Volcano. Hervey was a naval officer who served in the Seven Years War, rising to be First Naval Lord. Augustus Hervey's grandfather, the first Earl, was awarded the title as a reward for his support for the Hanoverian succession, formalised in the Act of Settlement (1701) which prevented Catholics from inheriting English and Irish crowns. Sarah Palin, Governor of Alaska and Vice-Presidential candidate during the 2008 President elections in the United States, named her daughter Bristol, partly after Bristol Bay.

54

Brislington has a Grade II listed nuclear bunker

The Bristol War Room was completed in 1953 and was intended to be a safe place for civil servants to coordinate civil defence and manage regional government in the event of a nuclear war. It was equipped with its own air filters, water supply and generators as well as 1.5-metre-thick reinforced concrete walls and could house the 50 people responsible for managing the defence of most of the West Country 7. Historic England, says the site is extremely well-preserved and was "built to the first nuclear-proof design intended for civilian occupation in Great Britain, and marks the strategic transition in the post-war British Government's appreciation of the effects of nuclear warfare".

55

Avonmouth has been home to Europe's largest wine warehouse and distribution centre

In 2021, Accolade Park covered 35.63 acres, only part of which is used for the storage of drinks. In addition to its storage capacity, the site also bottles an extraordinary volume of wine. According to the company, in 2021 the plant was producing a total of 1,200 bottles per minute and dispensing over 250,000 litres into cask per day. It was sold to a South Korean investor in 2017 for £62 million.

56

Lord Macaulay lived here

Thomas Babington Macaulay (1800-1859) is best known in this country as having established the "Whig view" of history. However, it is his influence on the development of the Indian legal and education systems that are his most lasting and controversial legacies. It was Macaulay's view that the British had a responsibility to mainstream western culture in India as part of a broader "civilising mission". He served on the Governor-General's Council in India 1834-38 and was instrumental in establishing an approach to colonial administration later known as Macaulayism, which prioritised English teaching over traditional teaching on the sub-continent. Macaulay was not a Bristolian but was born to a Bristolian mother and lived at Caledonia Place in Clifton briefly in 1852.

57

An 1171 decree gave Bristolians the right to live in Dublin

The oldest document under the care of Dublin City Library and Archive is a charter from King Henry II granting the citizens of Bristol the right to live in Dublin. He did this as an act of gratitude to Bristol's merchants who had financed his voyage over the Irish Sea to assert his authority over Ireland. There was a surge in interest in the document following the 2016 Brexit referendum; with many claiming this decree would guarantee Irish citizenship for Bristolians after Brexit. Unfortunately for Bristol, Ireland is no longer governed by England, thus the charter is not considered valid.

58

Bristol has the world's oldest Methodist building

John Wesley's "New Room" escaped both the Bristol Blitz and the redevelopment of Broadmead. It is now a Grade I listed and open to visitors who come from all over the world to see it. Apart from a central block of pews, the chapel is largely as it would have been when it was enlarged in 1748 under the instruction of John Wesley. A founder of the independent Methodist movement and one of the era's most important voices in social justice, John Wesley hosted many of the key Methodist conferences at the New Room. Bristol's trading connections with North America made it an important hub for the Methodists who went on to establish and build upon the movement in the United States.

59

Britain's first Labour Prime Minister was an assistant to a Bristolian priest

Originally from Lossiemouth, Scotland, the 18-year-old Ramsay Macdonald moved to Bristol in 1885. Influenced by the political radicalism of Scottish workers, by this point Macdonald already considered himself to be a Christian Socialist. Macdonald moved to the city to work with a clergyman at St Stephen's Church but he did not spend long here and moved to London in 1886. It was during his time in Bristol that Macdonald joined the Social Democratic Federation, Britain's first socialist political party, taking on responsibility for selling the party's newspaper.

60

Greta Thunberg led a march in Bristol

On 28th February 2020, around 30,000 people gathered at College Green in the centre of Bristol to see the 17-year-old Swedish environmentalist. Greta travelled to Bristol by train before making her way to College Green in a Nissan Leaf. After addressing the crowd, she then led a protest march in a loop around the city centre. Speaking outside Council House she told onlookers:

"We are being betrayed by those in power, and they are failing us. But we will not back down. And if you feel threatened by that, then I have some very bad news for you: we will not be silenced because we are the change, and change is coming whether you like it or not."

61

Leigh Woods is home to two Iron Age hillforts

In addition to three sites known within the City of Bristol area, the Dobunni tribe also built two camps at vantage points on the Somerset side of the Avon Gorge. Stokeleigh sits within the National Trust section of Leigh Woods and can be visited for free. The Burwalls (or Burgh Wall) camp obstructed the Victorian's development of Leigh Woods as a suburb in the late 1800s. What little remained of the camp was largely destroyed to make way for the housing that can be seen along North Road. Some of the undulating section of ramparts can be seen on the Nightingale Valley side of North Road, opposite St Ambrose (the residential home of the Catholic Bishop of Clifton), and near Burwalls House.

62

Only Fools and Horses was filmed in Bristol

Fictionally set in Peckham, South East London, the hit BBC sitcom was largely filmed in West London and Bristol. The Trotter's flat in "Nelson Mandela House" was actually a block in Acton for the first five series and then filmed out of Whitemead House (near Ashton Gate stadium) for the sixth and seventh series. A detailed tour of the other exterior locations used in the series has operated within the city. Another 80s hit sitcom, *The Young Ones*, was also filmed in Bristol, with the main house on the corner of Codrington Road and Broadway in Bishopston.

63

The HMV dog was a Bristolian

The image of a dog listening to a gramophone record is one of the most famous advertising images of the last century. Nipper (1884-1895) was a mixed breed Jack Russell terrier who lived with his human owner on Park Row. It was only after Nipper's death that his last owner Francis Barraud painted the famous image of him. The painting was called "His Master's Voice", which is HMV's full original name. A small statue and blue plaque attached to the Merchant's Building commemorates this world-famous dog, as does Nipper Lane in Kingston-upon-Thames, close to the dog's resting place.

64

Bristol is twinned with seven cities

Bristol is twinned with Porto (Portugal), Tbilisi, (Georgia), Puerto Morazan, (Nicaragua) Hannover (Germany), Bordeaux (France), Beira (Mozambique) and Guangzhou (China). Although "twinning" cities is a relatively recent phenomena, Bristol's connections with Porto and Bordeaux in particular go back many centuries. The Bordeaux Quay and Porto Quay areas of the docks are a testament to a trade in wine and sherry, which have been amongst the most valuable imports to the city since the thirteenth century. Both quays were named after the cities Bristol is twinned with, along with Hannover Quay.

65

Many of David Attenborough's best-known series were made here

The BBC Natural History Unit has been based in Bristol since its foundation in 1957. The unit has been responsible for a huge proportion of the world's nature documentary output. Several of these programmes have been the first to film particular animals in the wild and include landmark series such as *Life on Earth, Trials of Life, Blue Planet,* and *Planet Earth.* As well as the BBC's efforts, an array of smaller independent firms such as Silverback Films and John Downer Productions also produce content that is broadcast around the world.

66

The first mass-produced chocolate bars were invented and made here

The Fry's factory on Union Street developed the recipe for the world's first solid chocolate bar for mass production in 1847 and later the world's first commercially produced chocolate bar, the Chocolate Cream. The Cream continued as the world's oldest chocolate brand long after the merger with Cadbury's in 1919. Founded in the 1700s by Joseph Fry and benefitting from the triangular trade with the West Indies, the firm became the largest manufacturer of chocolate products in the country in the 19th century. By 1896, the company had around 4,500 employees.

67

The bodies of criminals were left on an island to warn off ne'er do wells

Dunball Island no longer exists. It was a 20–25-acre strip of land that lay off Avonmouth close to where Royal Edward Dock is today. In the 18th century the Dunball Island gibbet was erected to hang the bodies of criminals as a warning to sailors coming into the city that any crimes would be dealt with severely. The island gradually became attached to the mainland again before the construction of the Royal Edward Dock removed any trace of it.

68

The founder of Penguin Books was born in Bristol

Sir Allen Lane CH was born in Bristol on 21st September, 1902. Along with his brothers John and Richard, he founded Penguin Books in July 1935 aiming to bring affordable literature to the masses. Lane is best remembered for pioneering the use of paperback formats which reduced costs, thus increasing accessibility. In 1967 he founded a hardback imprint in his own name which went on to become a leading publisher of non-fiction works. The University of Bristol keeps a special collection of Penguin books and company archives, including 6,800 books from Allen Lane's own personal collection. Penguin's very first book was Andre Maurois's *Ariel*, now held within the university's special collections.

69

Somali was the third most common main language spoken in Bristol in 2011

In the nationwide census that took place that year, just over 5,000 people in Bristol listed Somali as their main language, while around 20,000 people in the city are of Somali heritage. The Bristol Somali Media Group tells us this is partly a legacy of the British colonisation of what is now Somaliland, as well as recent conflicts. In May 2013, Hibaq Jama became Bristol City Council's first Somali-born councillor when she started her term representing Lawrence Hill for the Labour Party. The second most spoken language in the 2011 census was Polish, fourth Urdu, and fifth French.

70

The "Father of Australian Architecture" was a West Country man

Francis Greenway was born in Mangotsfield (now BS16) in 1777. He went bankrupt in 1809, pleaded guilty to the crime of forgery in 1812 and was sent to Australia as a convict. There he was appointed as the first government architect and designed some of Australia's best-loved buildings. His portrait appeared on the first Australian $10 note, issued in 1966. His only surviving building in the UK is at The Mall in Clifton Village; originally built as a hotel, it now houses the Clifton Club (est 1818), and several properties in the club's portfolio.

71

Abraham Darby's pioneering work began here

Abraham Darby I is most closely associated with the iron foundry at Coalbrookdale but it was during his time at Baptist Mills that he began the work that would help start the Industrial Revolution. His company perfected new methods for casting brass, crucially applying sand to a new form of mould - an innovation we owe to his apprentice, John Thomas. Applied to brass cooking pots, Darby's Bristol brass works were able to produce a much lighter and thinner pot and became the dominant producer of these items in the country. None of the original works survived and the site now forms part of Junction 3 of the M32, but Know Your Place, Bristol has helpfully produced a 3D reconstruction.

72

The first Church of England female priests were ordained at Bristol Cathedral in March 1994

Angela Berners-Wilson became the first female Church of England priest on March 12, 1994. She was joined by 32 other women who became priests at the cathedral on that historic day. Angela's father had been a priest and she had studied theology at university. She went on to join the Movement for the Ordination of Women Priests back in 1978 and spent years campaigning for women to be allowed to take up the cloth. She later became chaplain at the University of Bath and prebendary at Wells Cathedral.

73

The *SS Great Britain* was the world's largest ship

Brunel's first ship, the *Great Western*, had been the largest ship in the world at the time it was launched. Now permanently housed in the dry dock she was built in, the *Great Britain* was twice the size of the *Great Western* but also had a more powerful engine, producing around 1,000 horsepower. She was the fastest way to get to New York at the time and is often characterised today as "the world's first great ocean liner". However, it was the ground-breaking combination of an iron hull and a screw propeller that has given the ship its much deserved place as one of the most important historic vessels still around today.

74

The comedian Lee Evans was born in Avonmouth

In recent times, Avonmouth is better known for its imports than its exports but in February 1963 it became the birthplace of Lee Evans, who would go on to become one of the UK's most popular stand-up comedians. In his autobiography Evans describes a time when his dad worked "on the bins" but, living above a doctor's surgery, he would occasionally pretend he was the doctor for the benefit of people queuing up under his flat. Before moving on to Essex, the family lived at Lawrence Weston council estate. Evans recalls: *"We were the dispossessed, continually ducking and diving in a generally hopeless attempt to make ends meet."*

75

300,000 Americans were stationed around Bristol in the run up to D Day

Much of the planning for D Day took place in Bristol, in terms of the overall strategy and in materials and manpower. Over at Ashton Court, Esme Smyth refused to leave her property, which had been requisitioned by the War Office and is said to have danced with GIs in the mansion's Music Room. Most remarkably, a Co-op on Whitby Street in Brislington was used as a storeroom for materials relating to the D Day landing. According to local historian Eugene Byrne, the Co-op also housed $20 million in francs as well as maps of anticipated battlefields.

76

Blaise Castle is mentioned in Jane Austen's *Northanger Abbey*

"Blaize Castle!" cried Catherine. "What is that?"
"The finest place in England-- worth going fifty miles at any time to see."
"What, is it really a castle, an old castle?"

Catherine never does visit Blaise. If she had, it would have been obvious that it is not an "old castle" but a folly built in 1766 as a place for relaxation. Austen lived in Clifton for around four weeks in 1806 but Blaise was in the hands of the Harford family at this time, with public ownership by the City Council still 120 years away.

77

Thousands of planes were produced under the name "Bristol"

The Bristol Aerospace Company produced some of the most important aircraft of both WWI and WWII. Its factory at Filton was the largest in Europe at the outbreak of WWII, churning out the Bristol Blenheim, Beaufighter, and Buckingham amongst others. The Bristol Boxkite, a replica of which hangs in the city museum, went into service in 1910 and is cited as one of the first aircraft to be batch produced. The firm moved into civilian aviation after WWII and was eventually merged into what is now BAE Systems.

78

You are allowed to beat carpets on Brandon Hill

Bristol's oldest public park was handed over to the Corporation (forerunner to the council) by the Earl of Gloucester in 1174. The Corporation sub-let the land for grazing up until 1625 when the site officially became a public park which is now thought to be the oldest in the country. 17th century Bristolians were granted the right to make hay, beat carpets, and dry clothes on the hill at certain times of day. Since 1625, Brandon Hill has been used as a defensive site for the Civil War, a meeting place for political movements, and a reserve for local wildlife, but it is the council's understanding that the carpet beating bylaw still stands.

79

Medieval monks established an underground water network for the Old City

Fresh water could be hard to come by in medieval times and although the science behind waterborne diseases was far from being understood, the importance of maintaining a clean water supply was known to the occupants of Bristol's Augustinian Abbey. The monks installed several wells and pipes that funnelled clean water around the city. You can still see St Edith's Well in Castle Park and a few markers show the route of St John's Conduit, constructed by the Carmelite Friars to pipe water from springs on Park Street.

80

Part of New York is built on rubble from the Bristol Blitz

Supply ships from the US and Canada steaming into Bristol during WWII brought vital equipment that helped keep Britain going during the war. The city had little to provide for the ship's return voyage but these vessels needed to be weighed down in the water to prevent them becoming unstable at sea. The best available ballast proved to be the rubble resulting from the Bristol Blitz, much of which was unloaded at New York port where it was used to form a new outcrop of land called "Bristol Basin". Commemorated with a plaque in 1942, this stretch of Manhattan includes part of East 25th Street and FDR Drive. Bristol born actor Cary Grant took part in a ceremony there in 1974.

81

Bristol was the first city in the UK to use electric trams

It is hard to imagine now but trams would have been a familiar sight to Bristolians in the early part of the last century. Bristol's tram network started off in 1875 with the use of horse drawn carriages and was upgraded to electric in 1895. Bristol Tramways was founded by Sir George White, who would go on to pioneer electric railways across the country and co-found the Bristol Aerospace Company. At its peak the city had 239 trains operating 17 routes. With the advent of the motorised petrol-powered bus, the trams fell out of favour and were gradually phased out from 1938. In 1941 a Luftwaffe raid on Good Friday took out the tram's power supply and the service was never restored.

82

27% of Bristol pupils were disadvantaged in 2019

The City Council's Quality of Life survey for that year stated that 1,320 children were allocated to a social worker, 629 were in care and 292 had a child protection plan. The 27 percent of pupils that the Council considered disadvantaged was around 16,900 children in all. 14,600 children under the age of 16 were from low-income families, roughly 17 percent of 16 children under 16. The 2020 Quality of Life survey also revealed four percent of households "have experienced moderate to severe 'food insecurity' in the last 12 months", whilst 19,600 households were estimated to have experienced fuel poverty in 2019.

83

The city was once enclosed within a medieval city wall

In common with most English settlements of the time, Bristol's original hub was enclosed within a city wall. Medieval Bristol had the added benefit of being surrounded by both the River Frome (later covered over) and the River Avon (later diverted for the Floating Harbour). The original Norman castle sat within the walls which would have had nine gateways and Bristol's "true centre" enclosed within. Only St John's Gateway still stands today but other sections of wall survive amongst the buildings of the Old City. The crypt of St Nicholas church contains a section of wall, as does the land belonging to the St Nicholas' Almhouses on King Street.

84

A historic Bristol pub is believed to have inspired two major works of fiction

The Llandoger Trow on Kings Street is widely believed to be the place where the writer Daniel Defoe met Alexander Selkirk, the marooned sailor whose life inspired Defoe's *Robinson Crusoe*. Selkirk spent four and half years marooned on an uninhabited island before being picked up by Bristol-born Woodes Rogers. Robert Louis Stevenson is said to have been inspired by the pub when writing *Treasure Island*, which features two pubs, The Admiral Benbow, based just outside Bristol, and The Spyglass, close to the docks and owned by Long John Silver.

85

There is a "named passenger service" from Weston-Super-Mare to London called *The Bristolian*

Originally in use between Temple Meads and Paddington, the route of *The Bristolian* was later expanded to include the service from Weston-Super-Mare. Other named passenger services operating out of Bristol have included the *Cotswolds and Malvern Express*, the *Merchant Venturer*, the *Devonian* and *Weymouth Wizard*. Few people now realise they are on a named passenger service as it rarely forms part of a route's marketing or travel information but you can still find yourself aboard the Bristolian today.

86

Brislington House was one of England's first "lunatic asylums"

The imposing Grade II listed Palladian complex later known as Long Fox Manor was originally built as Brislington House in 1806. It was a private lunatic asylum which at one time looked after John Thomas Perceval, whose father, Spencer Perceval, was the only Prime Minister to have been assassinated in British history. The lunatic asylums were forerunners to today's psychiatric hospitals and although their methods might not be considered useful today, Brislington House proved to be an influential model for other mental health establishments emerging in the Georgian and Victorian period.

87

Catbrain Hill is not named after cat brains

Along with a lot of South Gloucestershire, Catbrain Hill and the associated village was absorbed into Bristol (BS10) during the last century. Catbrain gets its name from the stony clay soil it sits on/ Known as "cattes brazen" in Middle English, this kind of soil will have been made for a poor area to grow crops, especially compared to more fertile areas nearby. Like many place names from this period, it has been gradually corrupted over time (think Brigstow to Bristol) and today it regularly appears in lists of the UK's silliest names. However, it serves as a reminder of a time when soil type was important enough to have an area named after it.

88

The last princes of Gwynedd were imprisoned in Bristol Castle

Bristol's Norman castle was situated in what is now Castle Park from the start of William the Conqueror's reign through to 1656. The House of Gwynedd directly administered much of Wales for eight centuries following the end of the Roman occupation of Britain. After the English King Edward I's conquest of Wales (1277-1283), the remaining members of the royal family who might have had a claim to succession were imprisoned in Bristol's castle for the rest of their lives.

89

Nevada's Bristol is entirely abandoned

Perhaps optimistically named "Bristol City" due to its proximity to the Bristol Range (of mountains), the site of Bristol Wells is now officially a ghost town. In the late 1800s, a small settlement developed to process silver which was dug out of the nearby Bristol Mine but the closure of the mines meant the closure of Bristol. Its post office shut up shop in 1950, marking the end of Bristol as an inhabited place. The remaining buildings were given protected status in 1972 on the National Register of Historic Places by which point the original settlement had been reduced to "the charcoal ovens, remains of furnace residue, and [one] original stone building".

90

Chew Valley Lake was created to provide water to Bristol

Now an important site for migratory waterfowl, Chew Valley Lake is an artificial reservoir, and the fifth largest in the UK. It was opened by Queen Elizabeth II, accompanied by Prince Philip in 1956, although it would take almost another two years to completely fill the reservoir which covers around 1,200 acres. Like many artificial lakes, its construction necessitated the submersion or demolition of pre-existing buildings such as the village of Moreton, which can be traced back to the Domesday Book (1086). Stratford Mill fared better and was relocated to the Blaise Castle Estate.

91

Bristol's first same-sex marriage took place between Mike McBeth and Matthew Symonds

The couple held a small ceremony at the Bristol Register Office on 31st March 2014 making them amongst the first in the country to take advantage of a change in the law which had come into effect on 29th March. A banner bearing "Just Married" was prepared by Mike and Matthew's friends and is now part of Bristol Museum's social history collection. The *Evening Post* carried a front-page splash of the couple kissing, which sadly proved controversial and resulted in a loss in sales.

92

The first modern bungee jump took place from the Clifton Suspension Bridge

The practice of land diving or “vine jumping” originates from the island of Vanuatu. It provided inspiration to two members of the Oxford University Dangerous Sports Club, who adapted the technique they called bungee jumping. The historic moment took place on 1st April 1979, when David Kirke dressed in a top hat and tails and, holding a bottle of champagne, jumped from the middle of the suspension bridge, shortly followed by Simon Keeling, Alan Weston (later a development lead at NASA) and Tim Hunt.

93

The M Shed houses a book covered in human skin

The council-owned museum is home to the book which has as its front cover the skin of the first man to be hanged at the nearby prison of New Gaol. John Horwood was hanged in 1821 for the murder of Eliza Balsum, with whom he had become infatuated and is said to have murdered by throwing a stone at her. A local surgeon, Richard Smith, dissected the 18-year-old's body in a public operation at the Bristol Royal Infirmary. His collection of case notes from the trial makes up the bulk of the book's contents. His murder conviction has recently been questioned and his skeleton, which for a time hung from a noose at Bristol university, was finally buried in 2011.

94

The Powder Houses stored gunpowder

The Powder Houses and Jetty are Grade II listed structures on the banks of the Avon at Shirehampton. Built in the late 18th/early 19th century, they were designed to house gunpowder from ships heading into Bristol Docks. In an era when wooden ships were tightly compacted into Bristol's docks and the city had a very limited capacity to control any fires that broke out, it was hoped that by storing gunpowder outside of the port the city authorities could avoid the risk of a major fire starting in the middle of the city. The house, which is now a private residential property, can be clearly seen from the public footpath on the North Somerset side of the river.

95

Fry's invented the hollow chocolate Easter egg

When you are next celebrating Easter you may want to spare a thought for the Bristol-based firm which gave the world not only the commercially available chocolate bar but also the chocolate Easter egg. Fry's launched the egg in Easter of 1873, at a time when Easter eggs were still decorated chicken's eggs. Other European countries had already begun to produce solid chocolate eggs at Easter but it was Fry's that perfected the technique for creating a hollow egg and introducing the practice of buying chocolate rather than chicken's eggs to the UK. Cadbury's, the firm that bought Fry's in 1935, has recently released a heritage reproduction of the original egg.

96

May Tanner was Bristol's first black ward sister

May Tanner arrived in Bristol in 1956, at a time when racial barriers to both work and housing kept many black people out of professional employment. Tanner worked at what was the Bristol Mental Hospital, and would eventually become a ward sister at the BRI. Princess Campbell MBE was long understood to have been the city's first black ward sister. Born in Jamaica, she moved to Bristol in 1962 and was the first black employee at the Wills factory. She received an MBE in 2011 and was awarded an Honorary Doctor of Laws from the University of Bristol in 2014.

97

Lawrence Hill is named after a leper hospital

Now a Bristol City Council electoral ward, the Lawrence Hill area derives its name from a leper hospital established by King John while he was Earl of Mortain. From the late 12th century onwards, the church had decided that anyone suffering with leprosy in England was best kept out of mainstream society, resulting in the establishment of over 300 leper's hospitals, usually based a few miles out from major conurbations. St Lawrence gained a royal charter in 1208 and ceased operations in the 16th century. Visible remains were still evident up until 1820 when the area was redeveloped and it is now thought the hospital would have existed roughly at the Lawrence Hill roundabout.

98

There were quarries on the Avon Gorge and Downs

This area has been quarried for centuries but mechanisation brought heavy quarrying in the 18th and 19th centuries, mostly for stone which was used as a building material. Many former quarries are still visible today, such as those on the corner of the Downs that backs onto Redland. The gorge still bears the scars of quarrying, most notably in the form of Black Rock, Gulley and Great Quarries. Many have been filled in with housing. At the top of Upper Belgrave Road, an area known as The Dumps was mined for lead deposits and the relatively small holes left by this process are still visible.

99

Bristol in Tennessee is officially the home of country music

Sitting on the border between Virginia and Tennessee, this Bristol developed into a substantial settlement during the 19th century. The state line is marked out with brass markers on State Street and the city officially, and functionally, operates as two separate entities. In the early 20th century, some of the first recordings of country music were made in the city and in 1998 the US Congress officially recognised Bristol as “the birthplace of country music”.

100

Isambard Kingdom Brunel was born on 9th April 1806

The youngest of three siblings, Isambard was born in Portsmouth to Marc Isambard Brunel and Sophia (nee Kingdom) Brunel. Marc was also an engineer and a refugee from the French Revolution, fleeing to the United States for six years from 1793, during which time he became Chief Engineer for New York City. Marc is best known for his work on the Thames Tunnel, the first tunnel under the river, now occupied by the Overground. Sophia Kingdom met Marc whilst working as a governess in France. Initially unable to escape the country, she was imprisoned by revolutionaries and accused of spying for Britain before finding safe passage in 1795. Sophia and Marc married on 1st November 1799.

101

Peregrine falcons have made their home here

Harmful agricultural practices and illegal persecution meant peregrine numbers crashed during the 20th century leaving many areas, including Bristol, peregrine-free. Thankfully, these birds are one of the UK's conservation success stories. The falcons returned to the Avon Gorge in 1990 and are now relatively easy to spot if you know where to look. A nest site is located on the cliff-face near where Circular Road reaches Ladies Mile. They are the world's fastest animal and can reach speeds of up to 200mph while hunting for other birds, typically pigeons. They have been known to fly into the city centre.

102

There's a piece of blitzed tram rail in the churchyard of St Mary Redcliffe

The Good Friday raids on Bristol were some of the biggest of WWII, causing huge damage to areas including Cotham, Knowle and Filton. A piece of rail protruding from St Mary Redcliffe's churchyard is a memorial to this raid. It is easily missed but a plaque beside the track reads: "On Good Friday 11th April 1941 this tramline was thrown over the adjoining houses by a high explosive bomb which fell on Redcliffe Hill. It is left to remind us how narrowly the church escaped destruction in the war 1939-1945." Winston Churchill visited the war damaged city on the following day.

103

Five people per week died of poor air quality in Bristol in 2019

Scientists at King's College London, the UK's leading centre for the study of urban air quality, found that around 260 people per year were dying prematurely of conditions exacerbated by poor air quality in the city in 2019. Their study focused on the prevalence of fine particulate matter (PM 2.5) and nitrogen dioxide, which can contribute to life threatening health problems such as heart disease and lung cancer. The same study also estimated that dealing with health conditions resulting from poor air quality was costing Bristol's health services around £170 million per year.

104

Whiteladies Road is named after a long-lost pub

Whiteladies Road was once part of the main route into Bristol from the Severn Estuary and today is one of the city's longest and best-known roads. How the road got its peculiar name has been the subject of urban myth and serious historical debate but it seems as though the UWE's Professor Richard Coates, who authored the book *Your City's Place Names* concluded that a public house that used to stand near the modern day Whiteladies Road was probably named after the snowdrops growing in the garden behind the building (white ladyes).

105

C S Lewis lived at Ashton Court during WWI

C S Lewis, the writer best known for the Narnia series, was commissioned into the Army whilst he was studying at Oxford university. He joined the Third Battalion of the Somerset Light Infantry and was posted to the Western Front in November 1917. Barely four months later Lewis was badly wounded when a British shell fell short of its target, killing two of his fellow combatants and leaving him with a punctured lung. Lewis was sent to convalesce on the estate, which was then a hospital for officers. He later wrote: *"Just after I was hit, I found (or thought I found) that I was not breathing and concluded that this was death...I felt no fear and certainly no courage. It did not seem to be an occasion for either."*

106

Bristol had a whaling centre

Whaling was a lucrative, if dangerous, business in the centuries leading up to the 1986 moratorium. Bristol did not develop a major interest in whaling, but there was a whaling station at Sea Mills dock between 1750 and 1761. A few vessels (Bristol, Adventure, St Andrew) successfully hunted whales in the waters off Greenland. Bristol's direct involvement in whaling closed with the end of this venture, but like much of the rest of the country it continued to benefit from whale-derived products for another two centuries. The Bristol-built ship *Liberty* (1787) took part in six successful whaling voyages before being lost at sea on the seventh. Canon's Marsh Gasworks (now flats) initially used whale and seal oil to produce oil gas for the Bristol Gas Light Company.

107

A Bristolian crew founded a Costa Rican village

The *La Tigresse* is said to have been unable to sail for nine days and nine nights after encountering a severe storm during the journey from Bristol to Grenada in the Caribbean. The schooner never reached the West Indies and instead beached upon Costa Rica's Limón Coast. There the crew found conditions favourable enough to begin a small settlement and named it after their hometown. In 1812 uprising of indigenous people resulted in the death of all but one of the settlers and the abandonment of Bristol, but a later Spanish colonisation re-established the settlement and it continues as a village to this day. A larger town further inland is named after Bristol's long-time port-city rival, Liverpool.

108

The Queen made her first post-coronation visit to Bristol in 1956

On 17th April, the Queen and Prince Philip arrived by train into Bristol Temple Meads before boarding the royal barge and setting out down the Floating Harbour, mimicking the route taken almost 400 years earlier by Queen Elizabeth I during her famous visit to the city. In a packed itinerary, the couple visited Charles Hill's historic Albion Dockyard, Lord Mayor's Mansion House and St Mary Redcliffe. They officially opened both the Council House building on College Green and the newly created Chew Valley Lake.

109

Brunel helped to protect the rare Autumn Squill

A nationally rare plant, the Autumn Squill (Scilla autumnalis) is more common on the Cornish coast than in our towns and cities. Its rarity was known to the Victorian enthusiasts of the Avon Gorge, who alerted Isambard Kingdom Brunel that the construction of the Clifton end of the bridge may imperil an important colony of this plant. Brunel ordered the plants be moved to a safe place; a translocation occasionally cited as the first time someone has moved a plant specifically for conservation purposes. In 2021, the Avon Gorge was home to three species of plant that grow nowhere else in Britain and seven species of tree that grow nowhere else in the world.

110

An old school building remembers the life of Thomas Chatterton

The remains of Pile Street School commemorate the life of Thomas Chatterton, sometimes referred to as “Bristol’s Shakespeare”. Chatterton was born at the school, where his father was a schoolmaster, and went on to become a prolific “boy poet” who inspired many of the Romantics before his death at the age of just 17. Today his early death is suspected to be an accidental overdose rather than the suicide that was presumed at the time. The school was largely demolished when Redcliffe Way was widened but a small section was retained, visible from the road.

111

Five Castle Park trees commemorate the Normandy landings

Planted in the 1990s, the Normandy Peace Garden is a memorial to, and a bi-annual site of remembrance for, Bristolians who lost their lives during the D Day landings. The five silver birches planted in the garden each represent one of the five sections of coast landed in June 1944: Omaha, Gold, Utah, Juno and Sword. The park also contains a group of cherry trees planted in 1986 to mark the bombing of Hiroshima, while another memorial recognises the lives of three Bristolians who died fighting fascism during the Spanish Civil War.

112

Gill Sans was developed for a Bristol book shop

One of Britain's most recognisable and widely used typefaces, Gill Sans began life as a shop-sign at 18 Charlotte Street (off Park Street). Its designer, Eric Gill had worked with Edward Johnston, creator of the famous "Johnston typeface" used on the London Underground and from which Gill Sans derives some influence. The original sign read "Douglas Cleverdon", the name of the shop's owner and original commissioner of the design. Gill was later asked to turn the font into a typeface, and it was soon adopted by LNER and put into use in railway signage, marketing and locomotive name plates across the network. Gill Sans was employed throughout WWII, including on the Keep Calm and Carry On posters. The BBC also adopted the font as its corporate text in 1997.

113

Black Boy Hill almost certainly derived from a racist place name

It has been suggested that the Black Boy Inn, which closed in 2021, derived its name from Charles II, who was given the nickname "black boy" on account of his hair. However, the most likely explanation is that the hill derives its name from the first Black Boy Hill Tavern, demolished in 1874 and previously known as Blackamoor's Head, a term developed in the Middle Ages to describe North African Muslims. After Charles II came to the throne, many pubs adopted the "black boy" namesake so it may well be that the evolution of this name is connected with the king.

114

The Downs is one of only three places to see the silky wave moth in the UK

A priority species on the UK Biodiversity Action Plan, the silky wave moth is a very rare sight but is thought to have had a stable population from the 1970s onwards. You may be able to spot the moth in the Downs or within the Avon Gorge in late June or early July. The caterpillars appear earlier and might be seen feeding on common rock-rose. It is the only place you can see this moth in England, its other sites being Great Orme (Caernarvonshire) and the Gower Peninsula (Glamorgan).

115

Avonmouth was the centre for WWI mustard gas

Mustard gas was secretly produced by both British and German factories during WWI. Under the orders of Winston Churchill, then Munitions Minister, the National Smelting Company at Avonmouth was established to produce the gas and HM Factory on the nearby Chittening Estate filled the shells. The factory would fill around 85,424 mustard gas shells during 1918. As well as causing horrific injuries on the Western Front, 1,100 gas factory workers, mostly women, reported 1,400 illnesses, while three were killed in accidents and four in associated illnesses. The filling factory injured over 1,200 women in just six months.

116

Bridgerton and *Poldark* were filmed in Bristol

The former seat of the Miles family, Leigh Court was used for many of the ballroom scenes of the Netflix hit *Bridgerton*, which also starred Bristol-born actress Adjoa Andoh. Released on Christmas Day 2020, it rapidly became the most watched series on Netflix. Leigh Court has also been used as a backdrop in *Doctor Who*, *Poldark*, and *Casualty*, the BBC medical drama which has a long history in the city. *Poldark* scenes have also been filmed in St Nicholas Market, Redcliffe Caves, John Wesley's Chapel (The New Room) and Ashton Court. Bottle Yard Studios on Whitchurch Lane provided indoor sets for the production.

117

There are 100 Grade I listed buildings in Bristol

Historic England protects certain buildings from major development or demolition if they are deemed to have "special architectural or historic interest considered to be of national importance and therefore worth protecting". Grade I is the highest level of listing. Some of the buildings are amongst Bristol's most recognisable landmarks such as St Mary Redcliffe, the Red Lodge Museum, and the Bristol Old Vic. Others, such as the city's three listed urinals, are less well-known. The entire Blaise Hamlet of cottages is Grade I, as is much of Portland Square in St Pauls. The Brunel-designed Avon Bridge at Temple Meads also features, as does much of the station itself.

118

Rocks in the Avon Gorge are 350 million years old

The gorge itself was formed relatively recently, towards the end of the last Ice Age, when the natural course of the River Avon was blocked. The river gradually cut through several layers of limestone and sandstone revealing a cross-section of rock layers that date back to the Carboniferous Period (358-298 million years ago) when this area was a shallow tropical sea. The study of the gorge was an important part in the development of modern geology and for a short while, the gorge was the namesake for a time period within the Carboniferous now known as the Dinantian. Sadly, few people now use the term Avonian to describe the time between 358 million to 330 million years ago.

119

There are no nightingales in Nightingale Valley

Bristol has two Nightingale Valleys, one is the National Trust-owned dry valley that adjoins the gorge near the Clifton Suspension Bridge, and the other is in Brislington. Sadly, neither valley now supports a nightingales. Environmental changes have brought about a 90 percent decline in the UK's nightingale numbers over 40 years and they are now mostly found in the South East of England. The Nightingale Valley in the gorge has, in recent years, been an important habitat for other threatened species such as song thrushes, bullfinches, and marsh tits. Brislington's Nightingale Valley is intersected by the Brislington Brook and has been known to support eels and kingfishers.

120

A riot on Park Street led to the death of an American GI

As the city did not impose many of the racial restrictions encountered by black servicemen in the States, Bristol was a temporary setting in the battle for race equality in the United States. Bristol did not enforce segregation and many black servicemen found they had new freedoms in Bristol that were not available back at home, exacerbating tensions with white officers. One of the public houses refusing to serve white and black GIs separately was the Colston Arms on St Michael's Hill. In July 1944, a protest over the issue of the treatment of black troops in the US military resulted in the death of one black GI on Park Street and the wounding of several others.

121

A Wellington bomber crash landed in St Andrew's Park (Bishopston) during WWII

On 30th April 1941, Vickers Wellington T2905 collided with cables connecting barrage balloons to the ground and crash landed in St Andrew's Park. Three of the six crew survived the crash. The plane hit a European black pine on the way down, taking off the top of the tree but leaving the rest standing and it survives to this day. A memorial in the park commemorates the lives of those who died in the crash:

61048 P/O. Kenneth Guy Evans
979838 Sgt. Thomas Leonard Lever
744913 Sgt. Charles John Clarke

122

The Floating Harbour took exactly five years to build

To get around the extreme tidal range of the River Avon, a section of the river was turned into a "floating harbour" through the diversion of the Avon and the installation of lock gates. This was a huge engineering accomplishment at the time, requiring the redirection of the River Avon down a 1.8 mile artificial waterway. This is "the New Cut" which runs past the Floating Harbour to the south. Work commenced on 1st May 1804 and formally ended on 1st May 1809. The navvies were who dug the cut were treated to a dinner on the newly formed Spike Island, but this is said to have turned into a brawl between English and Irish workers once the beer had run out.

123

Trees were planted on the Downs as boundary markers for cricket matches

In the late 1860s, the Gloucester County Cricket Club was in need of a pitch of its own and settled on a patch of Durdham Down. 16 beech trees were planted as boundary markers but audience numbers were not what the club had envisaged and W G Grace, one of the world's all-time greatest cricketers, had the matches moved to his old school, Clifton College, and then to Bishopston. The surviving trees are now known as the "Grace beeches". Check out the Bristol Tree Forum for more information on these and other trees, as well as advice on the trees in your own garden.

124

A Bedminster pub displayed a live lion to attract patrons

An outbuilding at the back of the Steam Crane on North Street (named the Bull at the time) was the scene of one of the most bizarre and violent episodes in the city's long history. To this day the exact details of what took place remain uncertain but we do know that in 1827, the pub's owner was exhibiting a lion (Nero) in the hope of bringing in more customers. One afternoon, a man by the name of Joseph Kiddle climbed into the cage to wake the lion for visitors who had been told they would see the lion in an active state. According to an account in the *Bath Journal*, the lion woke up more quickly than expected, launched himself at Kiddle who was paralysed by a bite to the neck.

125

Stone Age humans lived in Burwalls Cave

Head over the Suspension Bridge and down the hill past Burwalls House, you will reach the Burwalls section of the Leigh Woods National Nature Reserve. Donated to the National Trust by George Alfred Wills (who lived at Burwalls), this smaller section of the reserve contains a relatively large cave in which the Trust's archaeologists found substantial evidence of Palaeolithic occupation. It is just about accessible via footpath and is occasionally occupied by modern day Bristolians.

126

The tree at Whitetree roundabout is painted every year

Today's "white tree" is a lime that was planted in 1975 when the previous white tree died of Dutch Elm disease. This makes it the third tree given the designation of the "white tree" but no one is exactly sure how the practice of painting them came into being. It is possible that residents painted the tree as a guide for their friends making their way over the Downs for dinner parties. However, the most likely theory is simply that the tree acted as a convenient marker to help coachmen navigate the Downs.

127

The Ashton Court Estate used to be even bigger

Brought into Council ownership in 1959, Ashton Court is the largest public park in Bristol. Reduced to around 850 acres today, the estate used to cover Leigh Woods, much of Southville, Ashton Gate, Bedminster and large tracts of North Somerset. Many of Bristol's parks in the south of the city were purchased from, or donated by the Smyth family. Sir Greville Smyth Park in Bedminster was donated to the city in 1881 and named after him at the request of his wife, Emily, in 1902. Dame Emily Park is named after Emily Smyth, who along with her husband was the second-to-last private owner of Ashton Court and gradually sold off land as the estate became less profitable.

128

Marvin Rees was the city's first mayor of black African heritage

Elected as the Labour Mayor of Bristol on 7th May 2016, Marvin was not only the city's first black mayor but the only person of black African heritage to be elected mayor in any major European city. Born to a Jamaican father and a white mother, Marvin was born and brought up in Bristol, living in Lawrence Weston, St Pauls and Easton before studying in Wales and the United States. Marvin stood in the 2012 election which was the first to elect an executive Mayor for Bristol and resulted in the election of Independent candidate, George Ferguson.

129

Edmund Burke was a Bristol MP between 1774 and 1780

The Whig politician was a hugely important figure in late 18th century politics, both in this country and in the early United States. He is best known for his writing on political philosophy and although a Whig in his own day, he is widely regarded as having been one of the philosophical founders of "modern conservatism". He was noted at the time for supporting the grievances of the Thirteen Colonies, his opposition to the slave trade (which put him at odds with the city's mercantile elite), and the impeachment of Warren Hastings, a Governor-General of Bengal during the period of East India Company administration.

130

A Bristol nightclub is furnished with the interior of a Cunard ocean liner

The RMS Mauretania was launched in 1906 and held the westbound and eastbound transatlantic speed records for two decades. She was the largest ship in the world for four years and could burn up to 900 tonnes of coal in a single day. But for Bristolians the name Mauretania is also associated with a distinctive Park Street nightclub furnished in the ship's interior. Subsequently renamed, the club's interior has been lined with fixtures and fittings including the salvaged mahogany interior from the first-class passenger lounge and billiards room.

131

Newfoundland's first governor was a Bristolian

Born the son of a Bristol shoemaker, John Guy was part of a group of merchants who attempted the first settlement of Newfoundland. In 1610 he became the "first proprietary governor" of Newfoundland Colony which included Cupids, now regarded as Canada's first English settlement. Three hundred years later, the John Guy Flag Site was erected at Cupids to celebrate the tercentenary of the colony's founding. Every year an enormous 7 by 14 metre union jack (previously known as the second largest flag in the British Empire) is raised at this site. Christened at St Mary Le Port Church in 1569, he was buried down the road at St Stephen's Church 61 years later.

132

A woman from Devon convinced the city she was a foreign royal princess

When Mary Baker, a cobbler's daughter from Witheridge, Devonshire, arrived at Almondsbury in 1817, she did so under the guise of the fictitious Princess Caraboo. She spoke in a strange language no one could understand and engaged in bizarre rituals allegedly from a distant island nation. The Princess ended up at Knole Park where the Worrall family took care of her for a whole 10 weeks before she was rumbled by a former landlady. The family appear to have taken pity on her, and paid for her transit to the United States, where she took part in stage performances as the mysterious princess.

133

Bristol once had a thriving coal industry

The Bristol coalfield stretches from parts of the south and east of the city through to the Severn Estuary in the north. The seams that lie within the boundaries of the modern city (and county) are the foundations of a 400-year-old history of mining that took place in areas including Bedminster, Knowle and Kingswood. Mining in the Bedminster area can be traced back to the late 17th century and peaked in the early 20th century when many of these pits were owned by the Ashton Court estate. Some of these operations were substantial, with one pit employing 400 men and shafts descending as much as 300 metres, but there is very little left to remind us of this important industry.

134

Bristol is home to non-native wall lizards

The UK has three native lizard species: the sand and common lizards and the legless lizard known as the slow-worm. In the early 2000s, reports of lizards living around a garden close to the City Centre led to the identification of wall lizards (Podarcis Muralis), small black and green reptiles usually associated with North Western Italy. They're generally assumed to be escapees and can now be seen sunning themselves on the rocks and walls near the Clifton Suspension Bridge. The city is also home to another wall-loving animal, the tube web spider, a Mediterranean species that has founded a colony in the walls around Brandon Hill.

135

Seven species of tree are only found in Bristol

With only 150 species recorded in the IUCN's last assessment, the Bristol Whitebeam is one of the rarest trees in the world, found only in the Avon Gorge and Leigh Woods area. The other species are Robertson's, Houston's, Avon Gorge, Observatory, Wilmott's and Leigh Woods, whitebeams. They are all considered either endangered or vulnerable. In Frank Drake's excellent recent book, *Trees of Bristol* (Redcliffe Press), he tells us that the original Bristol Whitebeam identified by Martha Maria in 1854 is still there, just outside the ramparts of the Iron Age Stokeleigh camp in Leigh Woods.

136

A Bristol daredevil locked himself in a barrel that was sent over Niagara Falls

Charles Stephens, known locally as the Demon Barber of Bedminster, was West Street's notorious barber-turned stunt personality. He was not the first of the "barrel daredevils" to go over Niagara Falls but he was the first to die whilst performing the stunt. Stephens visited the falls in 1920 and against the advice of fellow daredevils, chose not to test an empty version of his barrel before launching himself off the falls. The barrel disintegrated on impact. Stephens' right arm, the only part of him recovered from the stunt, was buried at nearby Drummond Hills Cemetery.

137

Brandon Hill gets its name from St Brendan

St James' Priory was given the peak of Brandon Hill by the Earl of Gloucester in 1174, resulting in the construction of a small chapel. The Council-owned park, which today is home to Cabot Tower, became the site of a chapel and hermitage dedicated to a particularly important saint. St Brendan the Navigator is the patron saint for sailors, to which so many Bristolians made their way up the hill to pray before long voyages at sea. Her feast day is celebrated on 16th May. Today her name is associated with a sixth form college in Brislington, which has its own, more modern, chapel as well as St Brendan's Way in Avonmouth.

138

The Suspension Bridge was intended to have golden sphinxes on top of each tower

Designed during the "Egyptomania" period of Queen Victoria's reign, the bridge's towers mimic the architectural grandeur of Ancient Egypt. Brunel's original design included a sphinx on each tower and cast-iron hieroglyphs that would tell the story of the bridge's construction. It was not to be. The project ran out of money in 1843 and five years later Brunel was instructed to stop work on the bridge. He would never see the bridge finished and the towers never received the full Egyptian treatment but still derive a degree of Egyptian influence in their overall design.

139

The founders of Bentley Motors Limited attended Clifton College

Walter Owen (more often referred to as "W.O.") and his brother Horace Millner, were at the school in the early 20th century. Born in the London suburb of Hampstead, the brothers were sent to board at Clifton, where they were preceded by three older brothers. W.O. did not stay long at the school. Always inspired by engineering and the thrill of speed, he left at the age of 16 and went on to do a five-year apprenticeship with one of the country's railway companies Great Northern, before moving into aeronautical and then automotive engineering.

140

The world's oldest tugboat is in Bristol Docks

Now owned by the council, the Mayflower was constructed at a shipyard on Pooles Wharf and launched on 18th May 1861. She started out working life on the Gloucester and Sharpness Canal, before moving on to Sharpness Docks She was then moved to Bristol Channel and the Bristol Docks. Incredibly, the Mayflower was used right up until 1964, 103 years after construction. By 1977, she lay partially submerged at Gloucester Docks and the risk of scrappage hovered over the vessel until she was bought by the Bristol Industrial Museum in 1981. Today the Mayflower has a permanent berth outside the M Shed and is regularly used for steam trips around the docks.

141

177 Quakers are buried around Redcliffe Roundabout

From 1665 through to 1923, the area in front of St Mary Redcliffe was a popular burial site for Quakers. When the new roadway and roundabout was built, 177 headstones were moved into an artificial cave that now lies within a small park now known as “Quaker’s Burial Ground”. In the 1300s, this cave was occupied by a hermit called John Sparkes, under the patronage of Thomas Lord Berkeley, who paid him to pray for his health and well-being. Sparkes was required to live a life of solitude and pray for the health of his “master” frequently in return for food and shelter.

142

The Severn Estuary has the second highest tidal range in the world

With a range of 15 metres, Bristol's tidal extremes are second only to the Bay of Fundy in Canada, although it has recently been suggested the Ulgava Bay (also in Canada) may put the Severn into third place. The tides have caught out many vessels, particularly within the Avon Gorge, providing the impetus for the creation of the Floating Harbour. During spring tides, the Severn is one of only a few places in the world where a wave of water, known as a bore, is formed during the incoming tide. This can reach up to 7.5 metres in height and can be heard approaching from 14 miles away.

143

The Olympic Torch took a wrong turning just outside Bristol

The torch for the 2012 London Olympics took a momentary wrong turning, putting the relay half an hour behind schedule. The torch was carried over the Clifton Suspension Bridge and followed a route that included Hotwell Road, Southmead Road, Nags Head Hill, Old Market Street and Baldwin Street. 21-year-old Paralympian Blaire Hannan and Andrew Townsend from the 1992 volleyball squad had the honour of carrying the torch for the city.

144

The Lark Ascending premiered at Shirehampton Public Hall

Possibly Britain's most popular work of classical music, *The Lark Ascending,* was completed by Ralph Vaughan Williams at Kings Weston House (BS11) and first performed in Shirehampton in 1921. The orchestral version was first conducted by Sir Adrian Boult CH, who found himself in the city during the war years. The piece was selected by the BBC's Desert Island Discs listeners as "Britain's Desert Island Disc" in 2011 and was Classic FM Hall of Fame's No.1 track for three years running.

145

Philip John Miles was Bristol's first recorded millionaire

Philip Miles inherited and enhanced an impressive fortune amassed by his father, William Miles. A large portion of this wealth was derived from the triangular trade, specifically sugar plantations in Jamaica and the slavery abolition compensation pay-out as well as banking. In 1811, Philip Miles took over the Manor of Abbots Leigh (Leigh Court) with its 2,500 acres of land and demolished the pre-existing Tudor property. He later stood as MP for three West Country seats. His son, Sir William also became an MP and was the family's first baronet.

146

Bristol has over 100 miles of waterways

Bristol was built around the confluence of the River Avon and River Frome and evolved into a major international port because the Avon leads to the Severn. These larger rivers have had a major influence on the way the city has developed but the River Avon is just the largest of 12 rivers in the Bristol area (not counting the Severn), these are: the Boyd, Brislington Brook, Hazel Brook, Trym (hence Westbury-on-Trym), Siston Brook, Stradbrook, Wedmore Brook, Pigeonhouse Stream, Malago, Stradbrook and Frome. Many of these waterways are now underground or have had their routes restricted, but where they are above ground they often support small wildlife havens in the city.

147

Henry Overton Wills I was a non-smoker

The founder of the firm that would go on to be W.D. and H.O Wills (and the largest constituent part of Imperial Tobacco) is believed to have been a non-smoker. The Wills tobacco enterprise is well-known as having been a major employer in Bristol in the 19th and 20th centuries but the founding father of the family dynasty was not only a non-smoker but also not a Bristolian in the truest sense, having been born in Salisbury in 1761. It was his sons Henry Overton Wills II and William Day Wills who renamed the firm W.D. and H.O. Wills in 1830, and with the development of cigarettes, the brothers oversaw the firm's extraordinary 19th century growth.

148

Thomas the Tank was (partly) inspired by the GWR

The famous "Railways Series" in which the Rev W Awdry invented the character of Thomas the Tank Engine was first developed into stories when his son Christopher became ill and the family had run out of published books to read to him. Awdry had lived near the Box Tunnel (Wiltshire) in his youth and from there, he could hear goods trains being assisted up the incline by the local "banking train". He reimagined this childhood memory as anthropomorphised trains helping each other out in the first book in the series entitled "The Three Railway Engines".

149

Ashton Court contains the largest collection of ancient oaks of any estate outside of Windsor Great Park

Of note is the "Fattest Tree", a 700-year-old oak located by the path in the red deer park. It is one of several distinctive ancient trees in the park such as the Domesday Oak, a veteran tree on the pathway near the fallow deer reserve. This oak was named as one of the 50 UK "jubilee trees", chosen in 2002 as part of the Queen's Golden Jubilee and may be the city's oldest tree. The walk through the summer plantation is the best place to see many of the other veteran oak specimens as well as the estate's giant redwoods, which are also the city's tallest trees.

150

Bristol has the oldest continually-operating theatre in the English-speaking world

The Theatre Royal, now part of the Bristol Old Vic, opened its doors on 30th May 1766, back when King George III was on the throne. Opening night was not what you might have expected. The theatre was yet to receive a royal patent, making the first performance technically illegal were it not for the proprietor's claims that it would only be "a concert with a specimen of rhetorick". The theatre also did not have any front doors, so the first patrons were required to ask permission from a neighbouring house for entry to the theatre space.

151

Bartholomew Roberts sailed from Bristol

Roberts is often described as having been the "most successful pirate" of the Golden Age of Piracy (1650s to 1730s). He was born in Wales and the majority of his piracy took place off the coast of the Americas and Africa but his piratical career began aboard a Bristol slave ship (the *Princess*) in 1719. Roberts was serving as third mate on the *Princess*, which had anchored off the coast of West Africa, when he supported a mutiny by a fellow ship mate and was later elected leader of his crew. He went on to command a fleet of ships, one of them originally a Bristol-flagged vessel, and would capture or raid a further 400 ships, possibly as many as 470.

152

Belisha beacons are named after a Bristol student

Born in the London suburb of Hampstead, Leslie Hore-Belisha attended Clifton College where he was part of the dedicated Jewish boarding house known as Polack's. He served as a Liberal and then a Conservative MP, becoming Minister for Transport (1934-37) and subsequently Secretary of State for War under Neville Chamberlain. It was during his role at Transport that orange Belisha beacons were introduced to improve the visibility of zebra crossings at night. They can still be seen across the UK and Ireland as well as former territories of the British Empire such as Ireland, Hong Kong, New Zealand and Australia.

153

The Lord Mayor's Chapel is the only municipally owned church in the country

The official chapel of the Lord Mayor is located on Park Street and was once part of a much larger 13th century building known as the Hospital of Saint Mark. It was sold to the City Corporation (later Council) following the dissolution of the monasteries in 1541 and, following a period of use by QEH and the Huguenots, it became the Lord Mayor's Chapel in 1722. John Wesley was famously invited to speak in the Chapel in 1788 having been banned from the rest of the city's churches. It is a Grade I listed building.

154

Pero's bridge is named after a slave who lived in Bristol

John Pinney is the Bristol-based plantation owner best known in the city for having built "The Georgian House" on Great George Street, and for being the father of a future Mayor. He brought Pero Jones with him to Bristol in 1790. Pero and his sisters (Nancy and Sheeba) were made to work on Pinney's Mountraver's plantation (Nevis) from the age of twelve and would spend 32 years working for the family. Although referred to as a "personal servant" to John Pinney there is no evidence that he was ever given his freedom. When the new bridge of St Augustine's Reach was completed in 1999, it was the idea of Labour MEP Ian White to name the bridge after Pero.

155

Billy Butlin's first entertainment business began in Bristol

A Hoopla stall in Bedminster may not seem like the most promising start for a holiday camp empire, but it was here that Billy Butlin started his first foray into the entertainment business. The Butlins chain started a little later, in 1936. Butlin himself was born in South Africa in 1899 and spent time in Coaley (Gloucestershire), Bridgewater (Somerset), and Bristol in the early part of the 20th century. He briefly attended St Mary Redcliffe School and the Bristol branch of the family assisted with the acquisition of a travelling hoopla stall in the 1920s.

156

Almondsbury has a hidden Iron Age hillfort

The hillfort at Almondsbury followed a similar fate to the Leigh Woods (Burwalls) camp 60 years earlier. Discernible from aerial photography, most of the camp was developed when the owners of the Knole Park estate sold off their land in the 1920s. Knole Park House, which had been home to "Princess Caraboo" (the Devonshire imposter from 1817) was itself largely demolished in 1969, leaving only part of the property's distinctive tower. A brick factory and quarry was established on the site of a later Roman settlement (Cattybrook) which means some old maps incorrectly mark out the hillfort as a Roman camp.

157

D-Day planning took place at Clifton College

The upper school was relocated to Bude (Cornwall) during the Bristol Blitz, leaving the Clifton site empty. It was decided that the US First Army under commander General Omar Bradley would use the campus as its European headquarters, which it did from 1943-44, developing much of the plans for D-Day (6th June 1944) at the school. Sir Winston Churchill visited Clifton College in 1946, apparently saying to a student: “So, you’re the head of school are you? I was always the bottom of mine”. General (later President) Eisenhower gifted a signed copy of his book in 1951 and an American flag to the school in 1953 as a token of gratitude.

158

Bristol was one of the worst places in the UK to be young and poor in 2017

In the State of the Nation report for that year, the Social Mobility Foundation found that Bristol's youths were struggling to break out of the poverty cycle. One in four Bristolian children were growing up in poverty in 2017 and were likely to be hampered by poor quality childcare and low early years attainment. The foundation ranked local authorities by 16 different indicators for social mobility, with Bristol coming out 228 out of 324, placing it within the bottom third of councils in the country and behind the neighbouring authorities in Somerset and Gloucestershire.

159

The Smyth's family silver may still be buried somewhere near the estate

Thomas Smyth (1609-1642) is said to have asked for the treasures to be buried at the beginning of the English Civil War but neither he nor his steward disclosed its location prior to their deaths. Smyth was an MP for Bridgewater, and later Somerset, but had his seat taken away from him due to his Royalist sympathies. He fought with the Royalists but did not live to see the end of the conflict. His son was made a Baronet in 1661 following the Restoration, a lucky turn for Ashton Court, which could easily have been sequestered by Cromwell had Thomas survived.

160

“Shipshape and Bristol Fashion” refers to the strength hulls of Bristol ships

Before the Floating Harbour was created in 1809, Bristol’s docks were subjected to the full tidal range of the River Avon, leaving many stranded on the mudbanks for hours at a time. Being repeatedly beached and refloated with each tide puts huge stress on a ship’s hull, so Bristol’s ships needed stronger hulls than most. This gave rise to the shipshape and Bristol fashion idiom, a phrase which has subsequently come to mean general seaworthiness or to have something in good order and at its best.

161

Bristol City Council owns four ceremonial swords

Bristol's State Sword gets the most use and is placed behind the Lord Mayor during council meetings. It was manufactured in 1752, making it the most recent of the ceremonial swords. The oldest is the Mourning Sword, which dates from 1373, when Edward III's Great Charter of Liberties made Bristol a county - the first provincial town to be given this status. The Pearl Sword was fashioned in 1431 and the Lent Sword dates from 1459. In addition to the swords, the council maintains the ceremonial role of "sword bearer" (and deputy sword bearer) who carries the swords on civic occasions. Other civic insignia include the city's eight silver maces and a silver oar.

162

The Wills Memorial Tower bell is named after "three Georges"

The Wills Memorial Building was opened by King George V and Queen Mary on 9th June, 1925. The Great George bell at the top of the Wills Tower was named three different Georges: King George V, the architect responsible for the building Sir George Oatley and Sir George Alfred Wills, 1st Baronet of Blagdon, whose family money had paid for much of the building. At 9.5 tonnes, it was and remains the biggest bell in Bristol, the seventh largest in the country, and one of the world's deepest toned bells. It continues to ring out across Bristol to this day and can be heard from as far as 12 miles away.

163

The Ashton Avenue Swing Bridge was a double-decker

The Grade II listed building now carries the Pill Pathway over the New Cut near Greville Smyth Park (Bedminster). However, it used to be part of the railway line that connected the Bristol Harbour Railway with the Portishead Railway which runs through the eastern side of the Avon Gorge. When the harbour railway was still in operation, the bridge sported a central control pod to control the "swinging" operation, with space for a roadway to run under the pod while the freight railway ran under the road. An engineering masterpiece in its day, the bridge was hugely over budget when the GWR opened in 1906 but trains continued to use it right up until 1987.

164

Bristol Zoo Gardens was the first site in the UK to breed the endangered okapi

The Bristol Zoological Society was a founder member of the European breeding programme for okapi and since the 1960s it has overseen the birth of over 40 calves at both the old and new zoo sites. Okapi are the only living relatives of the giraffe and are rare both in and out of captivity. Native to the Democratic Republic of Congo, they have seen their habitat reduced by the expansion of human settlements and increasing deforestation. As of 2021, there are only 15 okapi in captivity in the UK and 100 in accredited zoos worldwide. They are listed as endangered by the IUCN.

165

Blaise Castle was built by a family with slavery connections

Thomas Farr bought 110 acres of the estate in 1762, having profited from investments in American plantations that used slave labour as well as rope-making. Farr commissioned Blaise Castle both as a folly and as a means of spotting his ships returning to Bristol. Farr went bankrupt in 1788 and the estate eventually ended up in the hands of the Harfords, who demolished the old property and constructed the Neoclassical mansion that is now part of today's public park. It became an unofficial base for the abolition movement. In 2021, Farr's Lane was still named after the family.

166

Hyacinth Hall was Bristol's first black headteacher

Born in St Mary, Jamaica, Hyacinth first visiting England in 1958, moved to Bristol in 1985 and took up the role of headmistress of St Barnabas, a primary school in St Paul's. She was determined to raise the standards of her school, notably refusing to open the school's buildings unless they were properly cleaned. Her spirit and vision continued to be a source of inspiration for teachers and community leaders well after she left the school and in 2004, Hyacinth was awarded an MBE for her work. She said: "It was the guiding principle behind my deciding to live and work in this country – to make a contribution to the country and also to Black people and to Black children."

167

Hyenas lived on the Downs

In 1842, workmen excavating a quarry near Stoke Road uncovered a cavern filled with strange bones no one could immediately identify. It turned out to be a collection of specimens from extinct animals dating back to the last warm phase of the Ice Ages, between 128,000 and 116,000 years ago. An account from 1887 has the cavern at around 90 feet long and containing the remains of a range of animals that are thought to have been scavenged or preyed upon by hyenas, who brought their remains back to the cave. Bristol Museum now houses some of this bone material, which includes fragments of grey wolf, hippopotamus, brown bear, cave bear, spotted hyena, small-nosed rhinoceros and straight-tusked elephant.

168

The Clifton Bridge was a collaborative effort

Although Brunel won the competition to design the bridge, its existence today is down to several people. It was a wine merchant, William Vicks, who first laid down the funds to pay for a bridge over the gorge, setting aside £1,000 in 1754. Thomas Telford, who had overseen the competition, thought a span of the whole gorge was too long, forcing the construction of the "abutments" that support the towers. Sir Greville Smyth, the naturalist and second-to-last private owner of Ashton Court, paid to have the road wide enough for carriages to pass each other. Following Brunel's death, the bridge was completed by the engineers Sir John Hawkshaw and William Henry Barlow.

169

Herbert Ashman was the first Lord Mayor of Bristol

Herbert Ashman became Lord Mayor of Bristol following the dissolution of the position of Mayor of Bristol in 1899. In November that year, he was knighted by Queen Victoria during her celebrated visit to the city. He would not have known it at the time, but this made Ashman the last person to be knighted by Victoria. Ashman had followed his father into the leather trade at the age of just 15 and would go on to set up his own firm. An advert of the period tells us the family were "leather merchants and importers" and "manufacturers of leather belts for all kinds of machinery". Nos 1-5 Broadmead still bears the name of the family firm Herbert Ashman & Co.

170

The City Centre gets its name from the tramways

The true "centre" of Bristol has long been the narrow medieval streets of the Old City, in particular the cross section of Wine Street, High Street, Corn Street, and Broad Street. Today's "Centre" got its name when the Bristol Tramways and Carriage Company began to use the middle of the city for their "Tramway Centre", hence "The Centre". The gradual covering over of the River Frome provided the firm with the space needed for the core of their network. Nos 1-3 St Augustine's Parade once housed the headquarters of the company and though the trams are long gone, the imposing 1897 Tramways Clock remains attached to the former HQ.

171

John McAdam lived at 23 Berkeley Square, Clifton

John McAdam is often referred to as the inventor of tarmac, which isn't strictly true but he is one of the most important people in the development of modern roads. In a process known as Macadamisation, his method for constructing safe, smooth, and efficiently-built roads was widely adopted across the world. However, it was here in Bristol that he first developed and used this process during his time as a surveyor for the Bristol Turnpike Trust. Utilising crushed gravel and stone as the base for the road surface, the roads laid down using his methods came to be known as Macadams, and when tar was added to the process, the surface came to be known as tarmac.

172

Bristol City Council planned to fill-in Bristol Docks

By the 1960s, Bristol's shipping was largely docking at Avonmouth. The council's ambitions for the inland harbour was to use the space to better manage Bristol's growing traffic problems and provide extra office space. Proposals put forward by the council in the 1980s included the filling in of the Floating Harbour and building a ring road in its place. A large section of Totterdown was demolished to form the easterly branch of this ring road but it wasn't to be - the council rejected the proposal by six votes.

173

The "Father of the English Hymn" lived at 4 Charles Street

Charles Wesley, the younger brother of John Wesley and co-founder of Methodism is best known as the writer of somewhere between 6,500 and 10,000 hymns. These include "Hark the Herald Angels Sing" and "Love Divine and Loves Excelling". He lived at Charles Street between 1749 to 1778 with his wife Sarah and his sons, Charles and Samuel Wesley, who were both considered musical child prodigies, with the latter nicknamed "the English Mozart". No. 4 Charles Street, is now a Grade II listed building and is used as an education centre.

174

Bristol voted 61.73% to remain in the EU at the 2016 EU referendum

Bristol was a majority "remain city" following the vote on 23rd June 2016 but a breakdown of votes by ward showed a huge variance in opinion on EU membership. In the Ashley ward, 86.6 percent of residents voted remain, and just 14.4 per cent voted to leave. This made Ashley the most pro-remain part of the city. Hartcliffe and Withywood voted 66.9 percent to leave, making it the most pro-leave ward followed by Hengrove and Whitchurch Park which voted 61.9 percent to leave. St George Central and St George Troopers Hill were both 50/50.

175

The first modern exploration of North America set sail from in Bristol

Although the precise site of their landing has never been definitively proven, the 24th June 1497 has generally been accepted as the date that John Cabot made landfall on what is now Newfoundland, Canada. The voyage was funded by a group of Bristol merchants and backed by a royal charter in the name of King Henry VII. To commemorate the 500th anniversary of Cabot's voyage, the British and Canadian governments decided on Cape Bonavista as the location of Cabot's historic landing.

176

The SS Great Britain carried the first ever English cricket side tour to Australia

Favoured for her speed and size, the *Great Britain* operated the Australia route for over 30 years. In 1861, she carried "the eleven of all England" from Liverpool to Melbourne where a quarter of the city's population turned up to watch. One member of the team, Charles Lawrence, decided to stay and played against the second English team to travel to Australia, also carried by the *Great Britain*, in 1863. Another Australia voyage saw the ship's cook adopt a Koala as a pet and on another, Captain Grey diverted the vessel to claim an uninhabited island for the British Empire.

177

The Knights Templar were active in Bristol

The Knights Templar are the best known of the medieval military orders set up to guard the Holy Sepulchre in Jerusalem and defend pilgrims on their way to the Holy Land. They constructed a round church on the site of the present Temple Church, which is understood to have been the administrative centre of the order in England's south west. They were active in the Bristol area from the 12th century but were suppressed in 1307 and their property in the city was handed over to the Knights Hospitaller. The "Meads" in Temple Meads refers to the water meadows that once surrounded much of the River Avon before they were drained.

178

Reginald Dyer lived here

On 13th April, 1919, a crowd gathered at a garden in Amritsar to peacefully protest the imprisonment of Indian pro-independence activists. Tasked with policing the event, Brigadier-General Reginald Dyer ordered his troops to block the exits from the garden and shoot until they had spent all their ammunition. The resulting massacre, later known as the Jallianwala Bagh (or Amritsar) massacre, was one the defining moments of the twilight years of the British Empire and helped to bring about its end. The exact number of people killed varies between several hundred to over a thousand. The disgraced Dyer later moved to a cottage in Long Ashton where he passed away in 1927, aged 62. A funeral was held at Long Ashton's All Saints.

179

111 species of fish have been identified in the Severn Estuary and Bristol Channel

Although it may be hard to see through the muddy waters, the Severn is thought to have the most diverse range of fish species of any river in the UK. These include dogfish, conger eel, cod, turbot, small eyed ray, thornback ray, river lamprey (rarely sea lamprey), herring, roach, brown trout, Atlantic salmon, dace, European eel, bream, carp, and sprat. Occasionally the estuary has seen unexpected visitors such as basking sharks and sunfish which are thought to have entered the river by accident. Dolphins and porpoises have been known to frequent the river, and the occasional whale.

180

John Lambton lived here

Lambton, later Lord Durham, was a significant Whig MP and colonial administrator. As Lord Privy Seal, he helped to draft the landmark 1832 Reform Bill and as a student he lived at Rodney Place (Clifton) from 1798 to 1805. As Governor General and High Commissioner for British North America (1838-39), he authored a report putting forward proposals for the union of Upper and Lower Canada as well as implementing a form of self-government. His model of "responsible government" would inform the treatment of some British colonies thereafter, a point underlined on a plaque at Rodney Place unveiled by the Prime Minister of Canada in 1933: "[his] famous report inspired all subsequent British colonial policy".

181

The GWR's Box Tunnel was the world's longest when it was built

Opening on 30th June 1841, the Great Western Railway transformed travel between Bristol and London, and at 1.75 miles in length, Box Tunnel opened as the world's longest. Brunel was determined to keep the GWR on the flattest gradient so the line avoids hills wherever possible. He felt there was no option but to tunnel through Box Hill but construction proved more challenging than he or any of his workmen had expected. The incomplete tunnel delayed the opening of the line by almost a year and 100 navies died during construction.

182

Wisconsin celebrates Elizabeth I's visit to Bristol

Every year starting in July, Bristol (Wisconsin) celebrates an event most Bristolians are barely aware of. In the summer of 1574, Queen Elizabeth I visited the city and whilst the original Bristol is happy to let this event pass by without much fanfare, the Bristol Renaissance Faire in Wisconsin takes over a 30-acre plot for an extensive series of events over nine weekends to commemorate the Queen's visit. With a mix of medieval re-enactment and outdoor pursuits, previous years have offered pirate darts, a Harry Potter-themed escape room, a giant duelling horse slide, archery, and a climbing wall.

183

A Westbury-on-Trym house is one of the earliest Modernist concrete homes

The Concrete House at 4, Ridgeway was the first in the UK to use Corbusier's "Dom-ino" system and one of the earliest homes designed by the influential architectural firm Connell Ward and Lucas. Their design might not seem radical to us today but it was an early proving ground for the open plan living that has become so popular today. The lack of any substantial changes to the property means it is now Grade II listed and highly evocative of the era it was built in. It must rank amongst some of the most under-appreciated of Bristol's historic homes.

184

Bristol petitioned against war with America

As had been the case at the start of the English Civil War, commercially-minded Bristol was keen to place business before politics. Bristol was the first city in Britain to forge substantial trading ties with the American colonies and had little to gain from the disruption that would come with war or a potential separation from the colonies. In a letter from 1775, a group of merchants, traders and manufacturers lobbied King George III to make peace with the colonists. The letter was presented to the king by the city's then MP, the Conservative philosopher Edmund Burke, but to no avail. Several Bristolian merchants went bankrupt as a result of the American War of Independence.

185

Rhode Island's Bristol claims to have the world's oldest July 4th celebrations

First settled in 1680, the New England town of Bristol is far smaller than the original city with a population of 25,000, compared with British Bristol's 460,000+. During the American Revolution, Bristol received two direct bombardments from the Royal Navy under the command of Captain James Wallace who burned down part of the town before turning on Newport. The Declaration of Independence was passed by Congress in July 1776 and Bristol began its official Fourth of July celebrations in 1785.

186

There are three "Brunel bridges" in Bristol

Brunel's "Other Bridge" as it has come to be known, was a swing bridge used in the Cumberland Basin between 1849 and 1968. It is located near Plimsoll Bridge which now carries traffic over the basin via the A370. Although the "Other, Other Bridge" is less well-known, if you use the Great Western Mainline, you may have crossed it more often than the Suspension Bridge itself. The Avon Bridge is a Gothic-inspired masonry railway bridge which carries the mainline over the River Avon into Temple Meads. Described by Grace's Guide as an "under-appreciated Cinderella of a bridge, a fine masonry structure hidden by two ugly sisters", it is one of Bristol's 100 Grade I listed structures.

187

Jacob's Well is believed to be the remains of a Jewish ritual bath

Jacob's Well at the bottom of Constitution Hill was once a source of natural spring water and the site of the remains of an important early medieval building. Easily missed by passers-by, the building is now believed to have been used for burial rituals (bet tohorah) where the dead would be cleansed before burial. Although the possible use of the site is still debated, it is a rare part of Bristol's medieval Jewish community, believed to have been established in the mid 1100s through to 1290 when the Edict of Expulsion was decreed by King Edward I, ordering all Jews to be removed from England.

188

Henrietta Lacks has a statue in Bristol

Henrietta Lacks died of an extremely aggressive form of cervical cancer in 1951. Unknown to her family at the time, some of the cells from her tumour were removed and became the first human cells to survive and multiply outside of a human body. Henrietta's cells (known as HeLa cells) made possible huge advances in modern medicine, including cloning chemotherapy, gene-mapping, the polio vaccine, and IVF. The cells have been used by research institutions all over the globe, including the University of Bristol, which commissioned her statue. Up until the unveiling of the bronze statue in October 2021, Bristol's only statue of a woman was that of Queen Victoria near College Green.

189

Henry VIII banned ferries crossing the River Severn from operating after dusk

With an extraordinary tidal range to contend with, crossing the Severn was not easy in a time before outboard motors and was particularly hazardous at night. In 1535, the king's ferry order decreed that Severn vessels would no longer be allowed to 'convey any manner of persons, goodes or cattalles after the son goynge downe tyll the sonne be up'. Henry VIII is thought to have visited the city in secret the year before this decree and in 1535 returned with Anne Boleyn for a retreat at Thornbury Castle and Acton Court.

190

Bristol was the first UK European Green Capital of the Year

The award, issued by the European Commission to Bristol in 2015, is one of many green accolades bestowed upon the city. The Jury were said to be impressed with the council's plans for investment in transport and energy, stating that Bristol had "great potential to act as a role model for UK, Europe and the world". In 2008, the city had come top of the Forum for the Future's Sustainable Cities Index and became the UK's first Cycling City, a £100m initiative aimed at encouraging cycling, of which Bristol secured £11.4m.

191

Eight people died in the Great Bristol Flood of 1968

On July 10th 1968, around two months of rainfall fell in just two days. The resulting floods claimed eight lives, including that of George Bowden, who died while trying to help two women out of the floodwater at Hartcliffe Way. The floodwaters damaged around 3,000 properties and put much of the transport network out of action. Trains stopped coming into the city and 24 buses were left stranded. Elsewhere, the occupants of above-ground flats provided accommodation for people whose flats had been flooded at ground level. Nearby, Pensford was severely hit, losing the bridge which carries the A37 and putting the Victorian Pensford Viaduct permanently out of action.

192

A village was destroyed for the Bristol Brabazon

The enormous but slow Brabazon proved to be a white elephant commercially, but an important project for the development of civilian aviation. To get the vast aircraft into the air, Bristol Aerospace had to extend their runway, requiring the demolition of Charlton. First recorded in the Domesday Book in 1086, the village had a manor house, a pub, a school, a few farms and its own post office. Although only one Brabazon would ever be produced, the extended runway did allow for larger aircraft to access the Filton site thereafter. The runway was closed in 2012 and new mixed-use sites (including Charlton Hayes and Brabazon) appeared in subsequent years.

193

In 1962, Avonmouth Dock workers refused to work alongside their West Indian counterparts

Between 10th and 12th July 1962, white dock workers downed tools in a protest against unloading vessels alongside black immigrants. By this point, migration from Britain's current and former colonies had brought thousands of people to the UK seeking work. Many were met with racial discrimination and abuse both at work and where they lived. Responding to the protest, the management removed 60 of its West Indian employees to placate its majority white staff.

194

Lead shot was invented here

One of the most improbable episodes in Bristol's rich industrial history took place in Redcliffe in 1782 when William Watts woke up one morning with, he claimed, the method for creating lead shot fully formed in his mind. To create perfect spheres of lead, Watts theorised that you could drop molten lead from a height, where it would take on a spherical shape, and have it land in a pool of water, freezing it solid. This in turn revolutionised traditional lead shot, which had previously been small bits of unworked metal, into the pellets still in use today. Watts' original tower was demolished as part of a road widening scheme, but the Sheldon Bush and Patent Shot Company shot tower from the 1960s at Cheese Lane survives.

195

Stalin’s daughter lived here

Svetlana Alliluyeva (later Lana Peters) led a turbulent life, of which her stay in Bristol is a small and little understood part. Her mother committed suicide in 1932 and her father died in 1958. Three of her own marriages ended in divorce and a fiancée died. In 1967 she denounced her father and his legacy, burned her Soviet passport and defected to the United States. After working as a lecturer in Moscow, following her defection Lana penned several best-selling autobiographies and attempted a failed return to her home country, ostensibly to look after her children. Peters says she was broke by the 90s, which is when she is believed to have been living in Clifton.

196

Harold Pinter's first play was performed in Bristol

Pinter was one of the most important dramatists of the 20th century. His debut was here in Bristol with a production of *The Room* in 1957, performed in the Wills Memorial Building by students in the university's drama department. Aged 26 at the time, Pinter wrote the play in just three days, partly as a favour to a friend, Henry Woolf, who needed to direct a play as part of his postgraduate work. One of the students who starred in the original 1957 production was George Odium, who played the part of Riley. While many of his contemporaries went on to roles in the media, Odium later became Deputy Prime Minister and Foreign Minister of Saint Lucia.

197

Easton was voted one of the coolest places in the world in 2019

In TimeOut's 2019 survey of the coolest places to live in the world, Easton came 35th out of 50 locations. TimeOut surveyed 27,000 people for their study, asking them to nominate the "best, most overrated and most undervalued neighbourhoods in their hometown". Lisbon's Arrios district topped the list followed by Shimokitazawa in Tokyo, Filipinotown in Los Angeles and Strasbourg-Saint-Denis in Paris. Only three other UK locations made the list, namely Kelvinbridge in Glasgow, Ancoats in Manchester and Peckham in London.

198

Bristol-educated Francis Younghusband led the 1903-1904 invasion of Tibet

The "expedition to Tibet" by the British Indian Army was motivated by the longstanding rivalry and distrust between Britain and Russia. Leading it was Francis Younghusband, who had started his studies at Clifton College in 1876. In common with other colonial wars of the time, the British military was equipped with Maxim machine guns and the resulting massacre of Tibetans provoked outrage in the British press, despite an eventual British victory. Younghusband was later promoted to Lieutenant-Colonel, knighted, and elected President of the Royal Geographical Society.

199

The University of Bristol's coat of arms recognises three historic families

The Wills family is represented by the sun at the top of the shield, a heraldic symbol which also appears in the stonework of the Wills Memorial Building. Colston is represented by a dolphin on the left-hand side and Fry (of chocolate fame) on the right with a horse. The centre of the shield shows part of the city's medieval seal of Bristol used by the city council (the ship and castle) and a book at the base represents learning. A 2018 study found that 85 percent of the wealth used to establish the university depended on slave labour.

200

Prince Albert launched the SS Great Britain, Prince Philip welcomed her back

The SS Great Britain was launched from the Great Western Dockyard on 19th July, 1843. She returned to the very same dock in which she was built exactly 127 years later, on 19th July 1970. In 1957, Prince Philip piloted a seaplane over Sparrow Cove on the Falkland Islands and spotted the abandoned Great Britain, which had been scuttled there in 1937. He became a major supporter of the project to have the Great Britain returned to Bristol and was on board as it was towed into dockyard in 1970. He later became the first Patron of the SS Great Britain Trust.

201

Bristol scientists were the first to analyse moon dust

The University of Bristol's Organic Geochemistry Unit, then led by Professor Geoff Eglinton, won the chance to be among the first institutions to receive and inspect moondust from the first Apollo moon landing in 1969. The team was tasked with assessing the sample for evidence of life. Included amongst its ranks was Colin Pillinger, the planetary scientist best known as the principal investigator for the Beagle 2 project. The 105 grams of moon rock was put on display and proved to be a popular attraction, with queues of Bristolians forming down Park Street. The team did not find evidence for life but did find evidence of methane.

202

Blackbeard lived here

Very little is known about Blackbeard's early life but it is generally accepted that he was born in Bristol around 1680 to a respectable Bristolian family. He would have grown up in the Redcliffe area and probably started out as a conventional sailor before becoming a privateer. He would have gone by a few different names (or aliases) but most accounts have him recorded as an Edward Teach or Thatch. In an intriguing coincidence, Woodes Rogers, (who offered Blackbeard the King's pardon, and led the way in removing pirates from North America's east coast), lived nearby on Queens Square. Blackbeard cultivated a fearful image, wearing a long black beard, occasionally adorned with smoking fuses.

203

Bristol Zoo's "Alfred the Gorilla" was stolen during a 1950s Rag Week theft

Alfred the silverback mountain gorilla arrived at Bristol Zoo in 1930 and quickly endeared himself to the public. After his death in 1948, he was preserved as taxidermy and relocated to the City Museum, where he remains today. In 1956, Alfred mysteriously disappeared from the museum, and was found on the Bristol university campus days later. Although presumed to have been a university prank, the truth of what had happened to Alfred only surfaced after the death of estate agent Ron Morgan several decades later. His family revealed the details of the prank as a tribute to Ron, who passed away in 2010.

204

Laughing gas was developed in a terraced house in Hotwells

Sir Humphry Davy set up shop at the Bristol Pneumatics Institute (6, Dowry Square) in 1799. Over the next two years, his practice became famous for its experiments into the effects of nitrous oxide, dubbed "laughing gas" by Davy who organised laughing gas parties with willing volunteers. Davy noted the potential use of the gas as both a potential hangover cure and for use during surgical operations. These parties were controversial in their own time, and had a reputation for being debauched, but the recreational use of nitrous oxide which began in Bristol has continued into the 21st century.

205

You&Meow was Bristol's first cat café

Opening in 2017, You&Meow on Denmark Street offered Bristolians the opportunity to enjoy their oat milk lattes surrounded by "feline zen masters". Shortly after opening, You&Meow won "Best Quirky Venue" at the inaugural Bristol Loves awards but also attracted criticism from animal welfare charities. The owner took the decision to close the café during the lockdowns caused by the 2020 coronavirus pandemic. Other Bristol cafes have featured swings and board games, whilst The Cloakroom on Park Row is a masterful reinvention of an Edwardian public loo and still houses many of the original fittings.

206

Bristol's only remaining tramlines can be found at Gloucester Road Medical Centre

Anyone familiar with the City Docks will be well-acquainted with the remains of the dockland railway which continued to carry freight right up until the 1970s. The tramlines shut down entirely when a power outage during WWII knocked out the network and little is now left of what was once an important part of the city's infrastructure. One place you can see the actual track in situ is Gloucester Road Medical Centre's car park, which has retained both the tracks and the cobblestones between them.

207

Washington helped capture Bristol for the Royalists

Prince Rupert's troops led a siege of the city, known as the Storming of Bristol, on 26th July, 1643. Colonel Henry Washington (a relative of the American President) fought on the Royalist side. There is a memorial to him at the top of Park Street, which marks out the rough location in which Washington successfully routed the Parliamentarian defences using just a small group of men. This manoeuvre has come to be known as "Washington's Breach". He is not a direct ancestor of George Washington but is connected through a common ancestor, Lawrence Washington. Two years later, the city fell to Cromwell's New Model Army, led by Lord Fairfax.

208

The Bristol Sycamore was the first British-designed production-ready helicopter

Designed by the Austria-born engineer, Raoul Hafner, the first Sycamore took flight on 27th July, 1947 from Filton. They were among the first production helicopters ever made, the first to achieve airworthiness in the UK, and the first to serve in the RAF. With a production run of 180, the Sycamores were deployed to armed forces in Australia, Germany, Belgium, and Austria. There are quite a few surviving examples around, including the Sycamore HR.14 XJ917, which you can visit at the Bristol Aerospace Museum, and two further models at the Helicopter Museum (Weston-Super-Mare).

209

The average speed of traffic on Bristol's A Roads was 15.9 mph in 2019

Between 2012 and 2015, a 20mph speed limit was brought in across the city, resulting in a drop in average speeds even on roads without the limit in force. In a 2018 review of the new speed limit, a majority of respondents were shown to be in favour of the change. A further UWE study indicated a 63 percent reduction in the number of fatal injuries associated with road traffic between 2008 and 2016. The report's authors suggested this may have as much to do with behavioural changes associated with driving more slowly as well as the change in speed limit.

210

Helen Dunmore was the first winner of the Orange Prize for Fiction

Now known as the "Women's Prize for Fiction", the Orange Prize was established to recognise the best full-length English novel by a woman. Helen Dunmore won the inaugural award in 1996 for *A Spell of Winter*. Dunmore was not originally from Bristol but lived here for most of her adult life. Her final book, *Birdcage Walk*, is a historical thriller exploring the lives of radicals living in Bristol at the time of the French Revolution. The book takes its name from Birdcage Walk in Clifton.

211

The Mayor of Bristol in 1771 was a slave trader who named a slave “Bristol”

Henry Bright lived at No.29 Queen’s Square where his house still stands. Like many of the merchants who lived in the square at the time, he had strong commercial links to the West Indies, specifically Jamaica. He was relatively rare in having a slave living at home with him, a man he named “Bristol”, and rarer still was the fact that he left part of his estate to his slave, specifically: "an annuity of £10 per annum, chargeable on the house where I now dwell, to my black servant, Bristol". The Brights continued to benefit from the proceeds of this estate long after slavery had been abolished.

212

Keith Floyd lived here

Best known as an eccentric television presenter, Floyd is often credited with having shaken up the diets of millions of Britons. Floyd grew up in a council house in Berkshire and his family later moved to Sea Mills. He took up a job with the *Evening Post* as a cub reporter soon after. Floyd's first bistro was on Princess Victoria Street, close to the Avon Gorge Hotel. His other two restaurants were on Chandos Road (Redland) and Alma Vale Road (Clifton). They were operational in the 70s and 80s but none proved to be a financial success. It was here in Bristol that he first dipped his toes into showmanship, as a chef on Radio West. It was also in Bristol that he met the television producer David Pritchard who would make Floyd a household name.

213

Slave owners were compensated when slavery was abolished

In 1834, the government paid out around £20 million to people who "owned" slaves. Based on 2013 values, the compensation payment amounts to around £16 billion and was 40 percent of the Treasury's annual income for 1834. These funds were invested in significant business interests, property portfolios, and political dynasties that would continue for decades. One of the largest single pay-outs went to Bristol-based Thomas and John Daniel who successfully won compensation for 4,300 slaves working on their plantations, netting £135,000, or around £9 million in 2017 values.

214

A future Prime Minister of India was educated at Badminton School

Indira Gandhi (Prime Minister 1966-1977 and 1980-1984) moved to the UK with her family in 1936. She had been to several Indian schools before moving to Bristol as well as being extensively home-schooled. She briefly attended Badminton; a fee-paying school situated on the edge of Westbury-on-Trym. Gandhi was the daughter of India's first Prime Minister, Jawaharlal Nehru, and following several ministerial roles, including home affairs, external affairs and finance, she became India's third Prime Minister in 1966. She was assassinated by members of her own bodyguard in 1984.

215

The first squid remains from Britain's Triassic were found at Parkway

Emma Landon of the University of Bristol's School of Earth Sciences discovered the first examples of crinoids and coleoid cephalopods from the Triassic period (251 to 201 million years ago) in Britain. These were found around present-day Bristol Parkway Railway Station in what the university described as an "unexpected discovery" in 2017. The crinoids are best represented by modern day starfish, sea urchins, and sea cucumbers while cephalopods include cuttlefish, octopuses, and squid. The Parkway specimens were over 200 million years old.

216

Roughly 55,000 Bristolian men enlisted in WWI

Bristolians played a significant role in WWI. The Douglas Motorcycle factory in Kingswood produced 25,000 motorbikes for the war effort, while Filton produced 3,000 fighter aircraft. Both Field Marshal Earl Douglas Haig (commander on the Western Front) and Field Marshal Birdwood were educated in Bristol. The City Museum estimates three million shells were made in the city and of the 55,000 Bristolians who enlisted, 7,000 lost their lives. A Bristol university medical student who single-handedly defended his position against a flamethrower attack was one of ten recipients of the Victoria Cross during WWI.

217

Thomas Lawrence lived at 6 Redcross Street, St Judes

Born in 1769, Lawrence was the foremost portrait painter of his day and a president of the Royal Academy. By the age of 10 the self-taught artist was supporting his parents who had suffered financial trouble as well as losing 11 of their 16 children in infancy. Thomas received his first royal commission at the age of 21, when he was tasked with painting Queen Charlotte. He went on to paint many well-known figures including the Duke of Wellington, King George III, and Pope Pius VII. He assembled one of the largest collections of Old Masters in the world and, following in the footsteps of Joshua Reynolds, he became Painter-in-Ordinary to the King (George III) in 1792.

218

Mansion House is the residence of the Lord Mayor

The Lord Mayor of Bristol is a ceremonial position which came into being in 1899 and is available to serving Bristol City Council councillors. Located on The Promenade (Clifton), today's Mansion House was built in 1874 for Alderman Thomas Proctor. Originally constructed as a private residence, he gifted (what was then) Elmdale House to the city in his will. The original Mansion House on Queen Square was burnt down in the Bristol Riots of 1831, and a subsequent property on Great George Street was later abandoned.

219

Eddie Hapgood lived in a notorious St Philip's slum

Edris Albert "Eddie" Hapgood was one of the best footballers Bristol has ever produced. He was born in an area known as The Dings in 1908 and would go on to captain both Arsenal and England. By the time Eddie was born, The Dings was arguably the worst slum district in the city, with many low-paid workers and their families occupying badly maintained and cramped housing constructed along narrow streets. Hapgood was initially signed up by Kettering (North Northamptonshire) and never played for a Bristol side but his tenure as captain at Arsenal and England covered a period of considerable success for both teams.

220

Dock wharves were named after cargo destinations

From the 1850s onwards, the City Docks established dedicated wharves for unloading of timber on Spike Island. Today's Baltic Wharf and Canada Way (from Canada Wharf, also a timber wharf), are a reminder of this trade. Elsewhere, the Welsh Back dock supported ships bound for Wales whilst nearby Finzel's Reach is named after Conrad Finzel's Victorian sugar refinery. Bathurst Basin took its name Charles Bathurst, a barrister and MP who campaigned against the abolition of slave trade. Underfall Yard gets its name from the dock's underfall sluice gates and Mud Dock gets its name from the mud.

221

A future Viceroy of India lived at 2 Bellevue Road

Between 1819 and 1824 this street in Clifton Wood was home to brothers John and Henry Lawrence, later Sir John Lawrence GCB GCSI (Governor-General and Viceroy of India, Lord of Punjab) and Brigadier General Sir Hugh Lawrence KCB. Sir John was amongst the first recipients of the Star of India and was made Governor of Punjab and then Viceroy after the Indian Mutiny in which his brother famously died. Three schools named after Sir Hugh survive in India today and two British public schools (Haileybury and St Paul's) have houses named after Sir John. However, he is said not to have enjoyed his years at the (now defunct) Bristol school he attended.

222

The King's Cinema was the first in Bristol to show a film with sound

Now the site of an office block called King's House, the Kings Cinema in Old Market had the distinction of being the first cinema in the city to show a film with sound, known as a talkie, with a showing of "The Singing Fool" by Al Johnson. Having been released in the States the year before, the film arrived in Bristol in 1929 and continued to be shown four times a day for five weeks. King's was operated by ABC right up until 1976, by which time it had taken to showing less reputable films and was finally demolished in 1981.

223

Warships were built in Bristol City Docks

The historic docks were an important shipbuilding centre for both commercial and military interests for several centuries. Many of these vessels had long and significant careers in the service of the Royal Navy, seeing action in the American War of Independence, the Napoleonic Wars, WWI, and WWII. Amongst many triumphs there were a few disasters. The HMS Saint Patrick was captured by the Dutch and repurposed as the *Zwanenburg* in 1667. The 50-gun HMS Nassau was wrecked off the Netherlands with 205 lives lost while the 70-Gun HMS Northumberland was wrecked off the Goodwin Sands and is now a Protected Wreck.

224

Bristol City Docks hosted its own Grand Prix

With the closure of the docks to commercial vessels in the 1970s, and the rejection of a plan to fill-in the entire Floating Harbour, attention turned to other possible uses of the harbour. One possible avenue appeared in 1972 with the advent of the Embassy Grand Prix, later known as the Bristol Grand Prix. From 1972 to 1990 the city hosted an annual spectacle of extremely fast powerboat racing, drawing as many as 200,000 people to the harbour. While today's vessels are limited to 5.2 knots (6mph) within the harbour walls, the boats taking part in the Grand Prix exceeded 100mph. The sport stopped altogether in 1990 following seven deaths.

225

Sir William Draper helped define the rules of cricket

Draper was chair of the 1774 committee assembled to refine the rules of cricket. The new rules are remembered for introducing leg before wicket and standardising the width of cricket bats. Lieutenant General Sir William Draper KCB was a key figure in the Seven Years War (1756-1763) which settled British supremacy over France in India. He is best remembered for having executed the capture of Manila (now the capital of the Philippines) from the Spanish in 1762. Manila Road, near the site of Draper's Clifton home, is named in recognition of this. His house is gone but Draper's Grade II listed memorial to his troops and a monument to William Pitt the Elder survive.

226

Ten died in the Dean Lane Colliery explosion

Bedminster expanded rapidly during the "coal rush" of the 1800s. Coal mining was one of the most dangerous jobs of the day and it is often said that as many as one man per month died operating the mines of South Bristol. The Dean Lane Colliery was one of the largest in Bedminster in the 19th century, with a contingent of around 400 men at its peak. On 10th August 1886, a gas explosion instantly killed a miner who fell into the pit. Nine further men died of suffocation shortly after. The youngest was John Brake, who was only 14 at the time. The site of the tragedy is now the council-owned Dame Emily Park, with a concrete hexagon to mark out the site of one of the shafts.

227

Bristol was a world leader in brass manufacturing

The British Isles lacked the knowledge and conditions needed to produce brass for many centuries. London merchants held the monopoly on brass importing and no one knew how to produce the metal with the raw materials available in the UK. That all changed in the 1700s when the Avon Valley area became one of the world's biggest centres for the manufacture of brass products. One of the principal sites for brass production was at Warmley (BS15), which also saw the first commercial production of zinc in Europe. The industry was heavily reliant on trade with West Africa and consequently declined rapidly following the abolition of the slave trade in the British Empire in 1807.

228

There were at least two Roman villas here

A villa at Kings Weston was discovered during the construction of the Lawrence Weston housing estate in 1947 and is now owned and protected by the City Council. Excavators got more than they bargained for when they found the body of a man inside one of the hypocausts (an underfloor heating system). He is thought to have died violently sometime in the fourth or fifth centuries. The Roman villa at Brislington was uncovered in 1899 and is thought to have been built in 270 AD. It boasted ten rooms, mosaic floors and hypocausts, and would have been one of the region's grandest properties at the time.

229

Netham Park was the site of a huge chemical factory

Although it is hard to imagine today, most of Netham Park (Barton Hill) was part of the 40-acre Netham Chemical Works, a sprawling industrial complex that once towered over the local area. The 91-metre-high chimney was known locally as the Netham Monster and the spoil heaps created beneath the "Monster" became an informal playground for local children who nicknamed them "the Brillos". Beginning in 1849, at its peak, the Netham works employed around 500 men, mostly producing washing soda and sulphuric acid and often in extremely challenging working conditions. The outline of the spoil heaps can still be seen but the "Monster" is long gone.

230

Mamma Mia! was written by a Bristol playwright

Both the play and screenplay for the first film were written in Bristol by Catherine Johnson, a script writer who had been working on the *Byker Grove* and *Casualty* TV series. Expelled from school at the age of 16, Catherine had an unusual career which included a brief stint at Debenhams in Broadmead and winning a Bristol Old Vic play-writing competition. When *Mamma Mia!* premiered in April 1999, Catherine expected to go back to "chasing the next commission". The play went on to be the ninth longest running show on Broadway, and as of 2020, was the seventh longest running show on London's West End.

231

A Brislington well was a site of pilgrimage for Christians

Saint Anne's Well draws water from a natural spring and is one of the city's few surviving medieval wells. Throughout the Middle Ages, the well, and the nearby Chapel of Saint Anne in the Wood, was a major destination for Christian pilgrims who came to venerate Saint Anne, mother of the Virgin Mary. The most famous of these pilgrims was arguably Henry VII who visited the well in 1485, followed by his wife, Elizabeth of York, in 1502. Not long after, their son, Henry VIII had the Chapel of Saint Anne dissolved as part of the Reformation and the building was later used to produce pottery. Today the well sits within a council-owned parkland.

232

4,000 people were buried in unmarked graves in Eastville

In Victorian times, the workhouse was developed into a means to provide the poorest in society with accommodation and a form of work but in an environment so unpleasant only the truly needy would end up there. With capacity for around 1,000 inmates, 100 Fishponds Road was the city's biggest workhouse. Between 1855 and 1895, around 4,000 inmates were buried in a mass grave just outside the workhouse. 743 of these inmates were children, 100 of them babies. 100 Fishponds Road was demolished in 1970 but the bodies remained. Their burial ground was forgotten until 2012 when it was discovered by the Bristol Radical History Group who campaigned for the former inmates to be memorialised.

233

City Museum has 650,000 biological specimens

The museum estimates that only 5-10 percent of their natural history collection is on display, with the rest being held in storage. This includes roughly 400,000 insects and 30,000 birds. Notable specimens include the Tasmanian Tiger (Thylacine) which went extinct in 1936. 786 Thylacine specimens have survived, most of them in museums or universities. The museum's Bengal tiger, shot by King George V during a visit to Nepal in 1911, was one of just 39 shot during one of the biggest royal shooting parties in British imperial history. The Smyth family were major donors to the collection, as was Bristol Zoo, which presented the best-known specimen, Alfred the gorilla.

234

J M W Turner painted the Avon Gorge

Turner was not long out of the Royal Academy when he embarked on a tour of Bristol and Malmsbury (Wiltshire) in 1791. He did most of his work whilst living with John Narraway, an animal skin dealer based in Bristol. The gorge became a particular focus of his, so much so that he gained the nickname of the "Prince of the Rocks". In the years before Portway became a major thoroughfare, the gorge was a source of inspiration for many artists and the importance of the area to Turner's early career was highlighted by campaigners when developers threatened to turn Leigh Woods into a spa town. His sketchbook is in the hands of the Tate but images can be viewed online.

235

Clifton traders used a tank to oppose a parking scheme

In 2014, Mayor George Ferguson attempted to roll out a new parking scheme designed to discourage people from commuting into residential districts. Clifton traders led by Tony Miles campaigned against the new rules which they said would undermine their businesses. To press home his case, Miles rented a 1942 Sherman tank and had it driven around Clifton with the slogan “Clifton traders defend their livelihoods”. It was not the first time a Sherman tank had been driven in the city. During WWII, hundreds of Shermans were parked on the Downs before being transported to Cherbourg via Avonmouth.

236

The country's first "poo bus" operated between Bristol and Bath

Fuelled by recycled effluent and food waste from Avonmouth, the Bio Bus (as it was properly known) went into service in 2014. GENeco, the Wessex Water subsidiary which provided the biomethane, worked out that a single passenger's food and sewage waste for the year would power the bus for a total of 37 miles. The poo bus boasted 30 percent less CO_2 emissions than regular buses and was the first of many such buses to go into the service across the country. GENeco went on to direct supplies of biomethane into Bristol's household gas supply.

237

A Bristol-based naturalist named 360 species of invertebrate

The Rev Thomas Hincks FRS was originally from Exeter and was a working unitarian minister before a throat condition started to affect his ability to speak. After moving to Leigh Woods, he dedicated the rest of his life studying the natural world. Thomas proved to be a prolific naturalist who not only named 360 species and subspecies but also named 24 families and 52 genera of invertebrate, and has an additional 13 species and six genera named in his honour. Many of his specimens are at the Natural History Museum in London as well as Bristol City Museum.

238

Soviet spies stole secrets from the Concorde project

Massive cost-overruns were not the only problem to plague the designers of (what would have been) the world's first supersonic passenger aircraft. Concorde had more than its fair share of Soviet industrial espionage with one Filton-based aviation engineer, known as "Ace", passing on 90,000 technical documents to the Soviet Union. Russia's TU-144 ("Concordski" in the British press) was completed and went into service before Concorde but proved to be a technical and commercial disaster. Following an accident at the Paris Air Show in which all the crew and several spectators died, the Tupolev was moved to mail services before being retired completely in 1984. Concorde continued flying until 2003.

239

Queen Elizabeth II opened Royal Portbury Dock

The Queen was on her Jubilee Tour of 1977 when she visited Avonmouth and granted royal status to the city's new deep-water port. The Royal Yacht Britannia arrived at Avonmouth Dock on the morning of 8th August where the Queen was accompanied by Princes Philip, Andrew, and Edward. Around 5,000 Bristolians were given tickets to see the royal family disembark from the Britannia for a tour of Bristol and its surroundings. Royal Portbury became a major asset to Bristol, described by Joseph Wilkes and Eugene Byrne as "an unusual tale of persistence and forward thinking by a Council never renowned for either".

240

The Bristol Bus Boycott led to the country's first anti-discrimination laws

In the early 1960s, the Bristol Omnibus Company was the dominant bus operator in the city. The firm operated a "colour bar", meaning it refused to employ anyone from Bristol's growing black and Asian communities.

In 1963, Paul Stephenson OBE, with Prince Brown, Roy Hackett OBE, Owen Henry, and Audley Evans, led a boycott of Bristol's buses which lasted 60 days. The boycott attracted national attention, succeeded in ending the colour bar in Bristol, and is widely considered to have helped to bring about the 1965 Race Relations Act.

241

Ernest Bevin lived at 39 Saxon Road, St Werburgh's

Bevin was a leading figure in the Labour Party for much of the early 20th century. Born in Winsford (Somerset) in 1881, he started working at Bristol City Docks at the age of just 11. It was there that he started to take an interest in the labour movement and formed his own branch of the Docker's Union. Bevin co-founded and then managed Transport and General Workers' Union, a powerful union body in its day, it later merged with Amicus to become Unite the Union. He went on to serve in Churchill's wartime cabinet as Minister of Labour and National Service (1940-45) and then in the Attlee cabinet as Foreign Secretary (1945-51).

242

Julia Donaldson went to the University of Bristol

The author of over 180 children's books, Donaldson met her future husband at the university and graduated with a degree in French and Drama in 1970. The author of *Stick Man, Room on the Broom, The Gruffalo,* and *The Snail and the Whale*, Donaldson was Children's Laureate 2011-2013 and was awarded a CBE in 2019. Dick King-Smith, another prolific children's author with more than 100 books to his name, lived just outside the city in the village of Queen Charlton. Best known as the creator of Babe, he was a teacher at Farmborough Primary School, a vice-president of the Avon Wildlife Trust, and was awarded an OBE in 2009.

243

The grave of a 18th century slave was desecrated by vandals in 2020

Scipio Africanus, an 18th century slave who worked at the Earl of Suffolk's residence at Henbury, is one of the few slaves to have any kind of memorial in the UK. Named after a Roman general, Africanus died in Henbury at the age of just 18 and was buried at St Mary's Churchyard under an elaborate headstone. In the summer of 2020, shortly after the toppling of the statue of Edward Colston, vandals smashed the Grade II listed grave site and left the message "put Colston's statue back or things will really heat up". The grave was restored after £6,000 was raised to secure its long-term care.

244

There are two "Matthews"

A replica of John Cabot's famous 15th-century caravel, the "Modern Matthew" was constructed in Bristol between 1994 and 1996. It commemorates the voyage that led to the exploration of what is now Canada. On the other side of the Atlantic, another replica was built at the same time at Cape Bonavista, now considered to be the most likely location for Cabot's historic landing on the continent. The modern British Matthew was launched into the docks by Lady Wills on behalf of Prince Philip, patron of the Matthew project, in September 1996. The ship left Bristol in May 1997, reaching Cape Bonavista on 24th June. It remains preserved in Bristol City Docks but its voyages are usually restricted to tours of the harbour.

245

An underground pipe network fuels the country's airports

Faced with the possible bombing of vital fuel depots during WWII, the British government authorised the construction of an underground network of pipes to supply fuel from Britain's ports to the RAF's airfields in the South East. The first of these started pumping fuel from Avonmouth in 1941 and is now part of an expanded network of pipelines supplying fuel across the country. Until 2021, coal was also imported into Avonmouth and distributed to the rail network via an enormous bulk coal terminal which dominated the Avonmouth skyline.

246

Bristol Blenheims were the first British aircraft in combat with Nazi Germany

Over 4,000 Blenheims were made in Bristol and they served in air forces all around the world, most notably during WWII. On 3rd September, 1939, within an hour of war having been declared on Germany, Bristol Blenheim N6215 flew over German territory as part of a reconnaissance operation on the German navy. The following day, a group of 15 Blenheims took part in the first offensive of the war, bombing German vessels in Wilhelmshaven. Several ships were damaged, but not sunk, while the RAF lost 24 crewmen in the raid. The last Blenheims were retired by Britain in 1944 and Finland in 1958.

247

Britain's largest aircraft was made in Bristol

Intended as an ocean liner of the skies, the enormous Bristol Brabazon had a wider wingspan than a Boeing 747 and was intended to carry around 100 high-paying customers in comfort and style. Bristol Aerospace's proposed designs included a cinema room, cocktail lounge, sleeping pods, and dedicated dining space. Initiated at the dawn of regular transatlantic air travel, by the time it was ready for service, the Brabazon was too expensive to compete with American alternatives and only one was ever made. The one and only Brabazon had its maiden flight from Filton on 4th September, 1949 and appeared at a few air shows before being scrapped.

248

Rownham Mead housing sits on top of an old dock

Shielded from the effects of the Avon's tidal range, the enclosed harbour at Sea Mills was the third "wet dock" in the country but proved unpopular with merchants. Originally known as "Champion's Wet Dock", Merchants Dock (1768) in Hotwells was built to accommodate 37 vessels. This also proved unprofitable and was taken over by the Merchant Venturers who, with a view to turning a profit as well as improving dock safety, sought a legal requirement for ships to unload flammable goods there before entering the harbour. It served as a dock and warehousing space up until its closure in 1965, after which it was filled in and later covered by housing.

249

An oil fire at Avonmouth killed two people

In the afternoon of 6th September 1951, the biggest peacetime oil fire on British soil erupted at the Regent Oil Company (now Texaco) terminal. Smoke from the colossal fire could be seen over 100 miles away which burned for several days and destroyed 6,350 tonnes of petrol. Two men died, Douglas Hyett, aged 33, and Arthur Charles Bagg, aged 38. Many more were injured. An investigation into the fire concluded that a mix of petrol vapour and gas oil as well as a build-up of static electricity had led to an explosion in one of the oil tanks, which in turn caused explosions in the nearby tanks.

250

Bristol mayors were direct beneficiaries of slavery

Those involved in industries that used enslaved labour included Sir William Daines (also an MP for Bristol), William Hayman, Henry Cruger (also an MP for Bristol), William Miles and Abraham Elton (of Clevedon Court, now National Trust). One of the country's biggest slave owners, Thomas Daniel, was Bristol mayor 1797/8. Sir William John Struth (Mayor 1814-15), owned estates on St Vincent and was later Governor of the island (1829-1831). Between him and his brother, Charles Pinney (Mayor 1831-32) netted £23,210 in compensation when slavery was abolished, around £1.4 million in 2017 figures. Some of this was used to build Camp House (later Engineers House) in Clifton.

251

A Bristol tugboat is now one of Malta's best dive sites

The MV Rosi was built in Bristol by Charles Hill & Sons in 1958, originally under the name of Rossmore. The Rosi was operated from Liverpool by Johnson Warren Lines Ltd and the Rea Towing Company but was redeployed to Malta in 1972. There, the Rosi was used as a tug in the Grand Harbour for another 20 years before Captain Morgan Cruises had her deliberately scuttled with the intention of creating an artificial reef for their safari tours. Submerged at a depth of 35 metres, the Rosi attracts a wide variety of marine life, making it one of the best-known dive sites off the coast of Malta.

252

There's a piece of Brunel's third and final ship at the Great Western Dockyard

Launched on 9th September 1859, the SS Great Eastern was an engineering marvel of its time and the largest ship in the world for four decades. Designed to do the Australia run it was a little ahead of its time and there was insufficient demand for its services. It found a useful role in laying the world's first oceanic telegraph cables. The ship suffered a major explosion on its maiden voyage, resulting in the removal of its forward funnel, a part of which is now in the Being Brunel museum, along with the ship's foghorn. Bizarrely, the mainmast is now a flagpole at the Liverpool FC football ground.

253

Henry VIII banned the fishing of eels in the Severn

In 1535, a royal order banned any catch of baby eels (known as elvers) for ten years to allow stocks to recover. Eels were a valuable commodity at the time and the estuary was an important fishery. The elver ban was upheld by Elizabeth I and overturned in 1778 during the reign of George II. It is thought that the European eel once made up as much as 50 percent of the biomass of fish in Europe's freshwater habitats, but their numbers HAVE declined drastically. European eels became a critically endangered species, subject to an illegal trade thought to be worth as much as £2.5 billion in 2020.

254

Seven percent of Bristolians said they had been a victim of racial discrimination in 2019/2020

Bristol City Council reported 1,902 hate crimes in 2019/2020, representing an increase of 177 percent on 2012/2013. In the most deprived parts of the city, the council reported 18 percent of Bristolians as having been victims of racial discrimination in the year to 2020. The data came from the Council's annual Quality of Life survey, which also found that 63 percent of respondents felt that they "belonged to their community", dropping to 18 percent for the most deprived parts of the city.

255

Hotwells is named after a natural spring which occurs in the Avon Gorge

The springs were leased by the Society of Merchant Venturers in the 1690s and attracted enthusiastic crowds keen to make use of the (alleged) healing powers of the hot springs, much as they would in Bath. Hotwells' peak as a spa retreat in the 1700s came to an end as the springs fell out of fashion towards the end of the century and in the 19th century access to the well was lost altogether when rocks were removed to allow larger ships to get to the harbour. The spring waters are believed to originate in rainfall at the Mendip Hills and at low tide you can still see part of the spring trickling into the River Avon.

256

Bristol City Museum has two Great Auk eggs

Sir Greville Smyth became one of the richest men in Somerset when he took over the Ashton Court estate. He used his newfound wealth to travel the world hunting wild animals and building a huge collection of biological specimens. This included two eggs of the Great Auk, a flightless bird that went extinct in the mid-1800s following centuries of human exploitation. Only 75 auk eggs still exist and two are in hands of Bristol Museum, donated by Greville's wife, Emily in 1910. Greville's collection was once stored in a separate "Bristol Natural History Museum" but this was badly bombed and most of it is now in the museum's basement.

257

Rhesus monkeys have escaped from Bristol Zoo

In 1934, 12 Rhesus monkeys escaped from Bristol Zoo's Clifton campus and dispersed around the city. It took several days to round them up, one made its way into a Clifton College dormitory and another managed to evade capture for an entire week before zookeepers were able to tempt the animal back with a trail of food. They weren't the only monkeys to find themselves in Bristol. When Castle Park's medieval sally-port (a secure entrance to Bristol Castle) was excavated in 1970, the remains of a monkey was found within the remaining structure. Now understood to be an Asian Macaque, the remains are kept by the Bristol Museum.

258

Brunel designed a pre-fab military hospital

More closely associated with wrought iron than wood, prefabricated buildings may not be the first thing we think of when Brunel is mentioned. During the Crimean War (1853-56), the British government commissioned a hospital that could be transported to Turkey and quickly constructed on site. Florence Nightingale dubbed the Renkioi hospital "those magnificent huts" and it is thought to have treated as many as 1,300 patients. Brunel's SS Great Britain served as a troopship during the war which saw Britain, France and the Ottoman Empire engage in combat with Russia. The SS Great Britain Trust estimates 45,000 troops were transported by the ship.

259

A Leigh Woods resident built a room for boxing matches with local gypsies

Arthur Way was the Eton and Oxford educated son of a local MP and first cousin to both Sir Greville and Emily Smyth. He is said to have developed a fascination with Roma culture during his time at Oxford and would go on to pen a first-person fictional account of a West Country gypsy under the pseudonym of F W Carew. He built a room separate to his main house which, according to the Gypsy Lore Society, was a place for meetings with "the fraternity" and "pugilistic activities". Later turned into a garage, it was incorrectly assumed to be part of a Smyth family hunting lodge.

260

Brunel is said to have smoked 40 cigars a day

Working a long time before the dangers of smoking had become established, Brunel's cigar-chomping was part of a deliberately cultivated image best portrayed in his famous photograph in front of the launching chains of the Great Eastern. Although his early death in 1859 is generally attributed to stress, Brunel's cigar habit can't have been good for his health. In 2011, Brunel's cigar case was sold by Bonhams for £26,400. The case carries Brunel's initials and the address of the Athenaeum, the Pall Mall club that counted Brunel amongst its membership. The case still holds one of his half-used cigars, believed to have been his last.

261

Mount Davis is named after John Davis of Hollywood

A 239m high hill on the western edge of Hong Kong is named after John Francis Davis, the second Governor General of Hong Kong (1844-1848) and the first Baronet of Hollywood (Gloucestershire). Davis had a difficult time as Governor. He was known to be "a friend of the Chinese" and a respected Sinologist who had translated several Chinese novels and clashed with powerful British merchants in the area. His Hollywood estate is now the site of the new Bristol Zoo campus but Davis's regency mansion survives as offices. Hollywood Tower also still stands, a 19th century observatory with a clock designed by Edward John Dent, who would go on to design the clock for Big Ben.

262

Bristol built London Buses

Red buses have become icons of the metropolis but some of the earliest London bus models came from a largely forgotten firm based in Bristol. Originally headquartered in St Philips, Straker-Squire opened a factory for manufacturing commercial vehicles at Lodge Causeway, Fishponds in 1907. The firm had started out in 1893 before the potential of the internal combustion engine was fully realised and its first models were steam wagons. They went on to produce 13 different models of petrol-powered cars as well as a few trucks. The company was responsible for the production of 70 percent of London buses in 1909 and later moved to London but the firm struggled to turn a profit and did not survive the 1920s.

263

Over 300,000 horses passed through the Shirehampton Remount Depot

The conscription of horses from Britain's farms was not enough to support the war effort as WWI dragged on. To make up the shortfall, horses were transported from the US and Canada and were prepared for combat at five sites in the UK. The Shirehampton depot was one of the largest, housing up to 5,000 horses at any given time. The depot is long gone but residents reported digging up horseshoes in their back gardens decades later. Around 484,000 horses died during WWI, roughly one for every two men.

264

Royal Edward Dock was opened by King Edward VII

The largest of Avonmouth's three docks, the Royal Edward, is an artificial harbour that had to be dug out and took six years to complete. The first shovel of soil was lifted in 1902 by the future King Edward VII in a practice known as "cutting the first sod". By the time the dock was completed he had ascended the throne and returned to Avonmouth aboard the royal yacht, "Victoria and Albert" wearing his uniform as Admiral of the Fleet and accompanied by Queen Alexandra and Princess Victoria. The yacht steamed into the dock on 9th July, 1908, cutting a ribbon on its way through. 70 years later, his great granddaughter, Queen Elizabeth II would open the nearby Royal Portbury Dock.

265

Sajid Javid lived on Stapleton Road

Born in Rochdale to Pakistani immigrants, Sajid Javid spent his school years in Bristol, where he lived above his parent's shop on Stapleton Road. Javid attended Downend School (1981-86) and Filton Technical College (later South Gloucestershire and Stroud College) (1986-88). He went to study at the University of Exeter and after a successful career in finance, which saw him become the youngest Vice President at Chase Manhattan Bank, he was elected as Member of Parliament for Bromsgrove in 2010. He held several prominent positions including Business Secretary, Culture Secretary, Home Secretary, Chancellor of the Exchequer, and Health Secretary.

266

Dinah Black escaped slavery to become a free citizen

Dinah Black had been working as a maid in the service of Dorothy Smith for five years when, in 1687, she was sold to a man who wanted to transport her to a Jamaican plantation. Dinah's first escape attempt failed, and she was forced onto a ship bound for the Caribbean against her will. The ship briefly stopped at Portishead and Dinah was able to escape despite having had her shoes taken away from her by the crew. She walked back to Bristol, and supported by local Quakers, Dinah took her case to the Alderman who ruled that Dinah was free to work, at least for the time being. Little is known about her life thereafter. She was included in Jane Duffus's *"The Women Who Built Bristol 1184-2018"*.

267

A Redcliffe slum was dubbed "Vermin Farm"

Large slum dwellings started appearing in 19th century Bristol as the city's population boomed and adequate housing stock was in short supply. Writing in 1884, the Bristol Mercury singled out an area near St Mary Redcliffe as one of the worst such areas, telling readers "there were almost nightly scenes of riot and tumult which could only be suppressed by the strong arm of the law." Vermin Farm was a term used by the police in the area who reported finding "8 to 10" people sleeping in the same room. Being close to the docks, the area was frequented by sailors in search of prostitutes, turning the church-owned land into an informal red light district.

268

A Bristol Type 138A set the world altitude record in 1936

Built at Filton, the Type 138 was a single-seater monoplane designed for high altitude flying. On 25th September, 1936, Squadron Leader F R D Swain secured the world altitude record in a 138, reaching 49,967 feet. Bristol Aerospace engines had powered altitude record-breaking flights previously, but the September flight was the first in a plane where the whole plane was built by one company. Swain suffered from oxygen starvation on the flight and had to break open his cockpit window for air when the plane descended. Variations of the Type 138A would go on to break eight altitude records.

269

Cabot Tower is built in Italian Gothic style

Although most of us know Cabot by his anglicised name "John Cabot", he was born in Venice and his birth name was Giovanni Caboto. To commemorate the 400th anniversary of his historic voyage, the City Corporation commissioned Cabot Tower and construction began on the anniversary date of 24th June 1897. The building is mock Italian Gothic and includes four Romeo and Juliet balconies that sit within Venetian Gothic archways. Mike Jenner, architect and author of *Bristol's 100 Best Buildings* says the tower "judged strictly as architecture [is] really rather mediocre but great fun and somehow lovable." It is council-owned and free to enter when open.

270

German Luftwaffe pilots are buried at Greenway Cemetery in Easton

The Luftwaffe launched a daylight raid on the Parnall aircraft factory based in Yate on 27th September 1940. Flying Officer Michael Royce of 504 Squadron shot down one of the Luftwaffe's Messerschmitt fighter aircraft which crashed into the courtyard of Manor Park Hospital (Fishponds). The pilots, Oberfeldwebel Hans Tiepelt (27) and Unteroffixer Herbert Brosig (21) both died in the crash. Theirs was the only enemy aircraft to crash in Bristol during WWII, and both crew members were buried at Greenbank Cemetery, alongside 26 other foreign national war burials.

271

St James' Priory is the oldest building in the city

Robert Fitzroy, the Earl of Gloucester and illegitimate son of William the Conqueror, founded the Priory in 1129. For much of its life the Priory was a home to Benedictine monks but like the larger Abbey of St Augustine (now Bristol Cathedral), this period ended with Henry VIII's dissolution of the monasteries 1536-1541. The original Benedictine priory was a much larger complex of buildings but today this remarkable Grade I listed church is the only part that survives. Now peculiarly positioned behind the central bus station, the priory can be visited on Whitson Street.

272

Bristol was the country's lead slave trading port from 1736 to 1746

Bristol was an early beneficiary of the end of the Royal Africa Company's monopoly on the "triangular" trade which saw vessels ship newly enslaved people from West Africa to the Caribbean and return to the UK with a cargo of sugar and rum. The UK's second city at the time, Bristol overtook London as the city transporting the greatest number of people on its vessels. It accounted for 40 percent of the British trade in enslaved people during this period before it was overtaken by Liverpool in 1746. Liverpool remained in this position until abolition in 1807.

273

In 1885, a 66-foot whale went on display in St Philips

Even before the advent of industrial whaling, large whales rarely made their way up the Severn Estuary as far as Gloucestershire. So when a fin whale beached near Littleton-on-Severn (Gloucestershire) in 1885 it became a major tourist attraction. Extra trains were laid on to cater for the crowds, some of which paid extra to meet the woman who first spotted the whale or even to have their haircut in the whale's mouth. The poor whale was towed into Bristol and spent a fortnight in St Philips before being disposed of. Incredibly, some of the whale's baleen (the part of the mouth used to filter small organisms for food) was rediscovered very recently in Bristol City Museum by curator Rhian Rowson.

274

Bristol City Council used Eastwood Farm for landfill

Much of what is today the east of Bristol was originally a series of South Gloucestershire villages that got swallowed up by Bristol as the city grew in the 19th century. Just as the city enveloped its neighbouring villages, it also grew around small pockets of working farmland that survived through to the 20th century. Eastwood Farm (BS4) is one such location. The farm was worked on up until 1971 when it was taken over by the council and used as landfill for seven years before being landscaped and repurposed as a space for nature. It has since become one of Bristol City Council's 12 designated nature reserves.

275

John Cabot brought back a huge whalebone from his voyage to Newfoundland

St Mary Redcliffe has one of the most interesting collections of artefacts anywhere in the city and an enormous whalebone, now supported by a stone cherub in the American Chapel, is surely one of the most unusual. There is some debate as to whether this was in fact brought back by Cabot or his crew from his famous 1497 voyage as there is no written record of that having happened. The Chapel is also the resting place of Sir William Penn (namesake of Pennsylvania).

276

Some of the last remaining "mounting blocks" are in Clifton Village

The ovular Pennant stone slabs outside the terrace homes on 8-31 Caledonia Place were used by the Victorians as steps to help them climb into their horse-drawn carriages. Only one other street in Edinburgh has retained these curiosities which are now primarily a hazard for car owners who open their doors without looking. The most famous resident of Caledonia Place is Lord Macauley, the historian and politician who left a controversial legacy in India through the reshaping of educational and criminal justice practices.

277

The Arnolfini art gallery used to be a tea warehouse

Arguably one of Bristol's most architecturally significant buildings, and certainly one of its most prominent, the Bush Warehouse started out in 1831 as a warehouse for the iron foundry Acramans. Designed by a local architect, R S Pope, it was the first example of the popular Bristol Byzantine style and was significantly extended for the company Acraman, Bush, Castle and Co for use as a tea warehouse. The innovative reworking of the building in the 1970s led the way for other sites on the docks to follow its lead. The Arnolfini featured on a Royal Mail stamp issued in 1984 with the heading "urban renewal".

278

Bristol trees are living fossils

Originally understood from the fossil record and believed to be extinct, living examples of the Dawn Redwood were found living in China in 1941. Subsequently planted in parks and by universities around the world, you can see some major variations of these at Oldbury Court, Woodland Road, and Overton Court (Leigh Woods). During the 2010 IUCN survey of this species, only 5,393 were found in China. The city has two examples of another endangered tree, the Maidenhair, which dates from the Jurassic period and can be seen at Canford Cemetery and on the Blaise Castle Estate. The many Bristolian examples of Monkey Puzzle are living specimens of another endangered species that dates from the Triassic period.

279

Like Rome, Bristol is said to be built on seven hills

The city walls of Ancient Rome enclosed the city between seven hills, leading to its nickname, the City of Seven Hills. The prominence of Rome in European culture has led to many large conurbations making the same "seven hills" claim even if the hills were outside the old city walls. Bristol is one of them, as is Bath and Bristol's old port city rival Liverpool. In 18th century Bristol, these hills were generally seen to be College Green, Castle Hill, the Old City, St Michaels Hill, Redcliffe Hill, Brandon Hill, and Kingsdown. The idea of Bristol as a "city of seven hills" remained a popular notion until the 19th and 20th centuries, when rapid population growth meant the city encompassed several hills.

280

There is a Bronze Age burial ground at Southmead

The Round Barrow in Badock's Wood is thought to be around 3,300 years old. Gifted to the city by local industrialist Sir Stanley Badock and protected by a covenant with the Council, Badock's Wood has become a natural oasis and is one of the city's 12 designated nature reserves. The Round Barrow was partially excavated in 1873, revealing a mound consisting of "small unshaped stones of carboniferous limestone carefully piled up and embedded in a reddish earth", as well as animal and human bones and flint scrapers. It is now marked by a monument commissioned in 2002 by Bristol City Council to clearly indicate the significance of the site and deter vandalism.

281

Darth Vader was a Bristolian

Surely every Bristolian's favourite fact, it is well known that David Prowse MBE was chosen by George Lucas to provide the physical presence of Darth Vader in the original *Star Wars* trilogy. Prowse was born in Bristol; he grew up on a council estate in Southmead and obtained a scholarship to Bristol Grammar School. He would go on to win the British weightlifting championship in 1962, 63 and 64. At six foot and six inches, David's physique provided the stature needed for Vader's menacing role. James Earl Jones was brought in to provide a more sinister voiceover for Darth Vader, while Prowse's own West Country accent would lead to the on-set nickname "Darth Farmer".

282

Two Bristol brothers established the first English Channel submarine cable

Jacob and John Watkins Brett were sons of a Bristol-based cabinet maker William Brett. In 1850, they laid the first undersea cable from Dover to Calais (which snagged and split by a fishing boat), followed by another working cable in 1851. To mark the occasion, a signal was sent from Dover to Calais, setting off a cannon at the other end. It was a landmark moment in both communications and Anglo-French relations and the first time an undersea cable had been successfully installed. The technology spread rapidly thereafter.

283

The Bristol Sweet Mart was founded by Ugandan refugees

The success of the Bristol Sweet Mart represents an extraordinary reversal in fortunes for the company's founder, Kassam Ismail Majothi. In 1972, Kassam, his wife, and their six children were amongst thousands of Indians forced to flee Idi Amin's Uganda. They abandoned not only their homes but their original business, and soon found themselves living in a refugee camp at Watchet, Somerset. The Sweet Mart opened its doors in 1978 and four decades later, the family firm is thriving, boasting in 2021 of being "the largest provider of ethnic foods and spices in the South West".

284

Leigh Woods was nearly turned into a spa town

The Smyth family added the Leigh Woods area to the Ashton Court estate in 1605. Two and a half centuries later, the completion of the suspension bridge meant Leigh Woods was easily accessible from Clifton and could be developed into a "small spa town". Plans were drawn up for hundreds of homes, a hotel and a bridge over Nightingale Valley. Significant opposition mounted in both the local and national press and the land was eventually acquired by the Leigh Woods Land Company, a firm established by a group of wealthy Bristolians who allowed for a more partial development. In 1909, George Alfred Wills bought the remaining land and donated it to the National Trust.

285

Eleven Bristol MPs benefited directly from slave ownership compensation

The Bristol constituency was a two-person seat in the House of Commons from 1295 to 1885. Following the abolition of slavery in the British Empire, at least eleven of its 19th century MPs were direct beneficiaries of the Abolition Act and appear on UCL's Legacies of British Slave-ownership database. This is just one of the ways in which we can assess the legacy of slavery. Many MPs from before this period, such as Edward Colston, derived their wealth from slavery and many others since will have benefitted in less tangible, or unrecorded ways.

286

The International Movie Database (IMDb) was started in Stoke Gifford

One of the most successful websites in the world, IMDb was started as a hobby by then-Hewlett-Packard employee and self-confessed film buff Colin Needham in 1990. Initially launched as a database that needed to be downloaded for access, it was one of the first 100 websites to be launched in 1993 and became Amazon's first ever acquisition in 1998. By 2017 it was attracting 250 million monthly users and a year later, Colin was awarded with an honorary degree from the University of Bristol.

287

A Bristolian secured the Guinness World Record for the longest wheelchair basketball marathon

Other Guinness World Records secured by Bristolians include: the greatest distance travelled on a space hopper, the largest paper shopping bag, the oldest person to receive an honorary degree, most consecutive pull ups with a ball balanced on the head, fastest half marathon dressed as a cartoon character, longest marathon ironing, largest gathering of people dressed as astronauts, most skips on a tightrope in one minute, and the most BMX death truck spins in one minute.

288

Mya-Rose Craig held the world's most northerly climate protest

The ornithologist from Compton Martin had observed half the world's bird species by the time she reached her mid-teens. Better known as Birdgirl, aged just 18, she travelled to the edge of the Arctic ice sheet (82.2° North) aboard the Greenpeace vessel *Arctic Sunrise* and held a climate protest on an ice floe. The year before (2019), Mya is understood to have become the youngest person in the UK to receive an honorary degree (University of Bristol) and was included in the BBC Radio Four Woman's Hour Power List 2020.

289

Bristol was one the UK's most unequal cities in the early 2000s

A report by the Centre on Dynamics for Ethnicity and the Runnymede Trust found that "Ethnic minorities in Bristol experience greater disadvantage than in England and Wales as a whole in education and employment and this is particularly so for Black African people". The report, entitled, "Bristol: a city divided?" (2017) drew on census data (2001 and 2011) as well as information gathered from workshops with local organisations. It was noted that Bristol was 7th out of 348 districts considered for the Multiple Inequality Index, with 1st being the worst district.

290

Albion Rajkumar Banerjee was the first Bengali Brahmo born in Britain

Named after a Celtic word for Britain, Albion Rajkumar Banerjee was born at Red Lodge on 10th October 1871. The lodge was then owned by the social reformer Mary Carpenter, who wrote to Queen Victoria's private secretary believing (incorrectly) that Albion was the first British-born Indian. He followed a reformist monotheistic Hindu movement known as Brahmoism. Having joined the Indian Civil Service, Albion would go on to become Diwan of Cochin (1907-1914), Diwan of Mysore (1922-1926) and Prime Minister of Kashmir (1927-1929). He was knighted in 1925.

291

Isaac Rosenberg was born in Bristol

Rosenberg was the son of working-class Jewish refugees who had settled in Bristol's Temple district. He served in the trenches and lost his life fighting near Arras but not before he had penned some of the great poems of WWI. On Armistice Day 1985, Rosenberg was one of 16 war poets to be commemorated on a slate plaque at Westminster Abbey.

A man's brains splattered on
A stretcher-bearer's face;
His shook shoulders slipped their load,
But when they bent to look again
The drowning soul was sunk too deep
For human tenderness.

292

An Emperor of Ethiopia was a regular at Weston's outdoor swimming pool

Emperor Haile Selassie I was forced to leave Ethiopia in 1936 when his country was invaded by Mussolini's Italy. He lived in exile at Fairfield House in Bath until 1941 and later gifted the house to the city for use as an old people's home. The outdoor swimming pool (later Tropicana) at Weston-Super-Mare may not be somewhere you would expect to find an Ethiopian emperor, but it became his favourite swimming spot and he is said to have been happy queuing up for a swim with the other visitors. In 2019, UWE Bristol funded the first official blue plaque in Bath, recognising his time at Fairfield House.

293

The Open Arms used to be called the Colston Arms

The pub on St Michael's Hill was one of many Bristol establishments that underwent a name change following the tearing down of Edward Colston's statue in theCity Centre. Colston was a Bristol-born 17th century merchant, slave trader and MP for Bristol who was widely celebrated in Bristol on account of his philanthropy. Views towards his legacy started to change in the early 2000s and the Colston Arms was temporarily renamed "Ye olde Pubby Mcdrunkface" in 2020, before finally settling on Open Arms towards the end of 2021. Other name changes included the Colston Tower (Beacon Tower), Colston Hall (Bristol Beacon) and Colston's Girls' School (Montpelier High School).

294

Bristol was repeatedly hit by outbreaks of "The Plague"

From the 1300s through to the 1600s, Britain was hit by waves of bubonic plague. Very little is known about life in Bristol during these episodes but a good overview of some of the worst outbreaks has been compiled in the Post by Eugene Byrne. An account of the "Black Death" of 1348-49 suggests that most of Bristol's population died. In 1564, 2,500 people are believed to have died in another outbreak (around one quarter of the city's population) and in 1603-1606 the plague returned and wiped out 2,600 Bristolians. During the Covid-19 pandemic, a Black Death-inspired board game called Bristol 1350 raised £726,705 in crowd funding and sold thousands of copies.

295

St Mary Redcliffe's "pipe walk" is one of the oldest customs in the city

In the 12th century, the feudal baron Robert de Berkeley donated a water source to the city. This consisted of a well in what is now Knowle and a manmade conduit that provides a flow of water to Redcliffe. The St Mary Redcliffe pipe begins in what is now an allotment garden, and follows the ancient route for two miles to St Mary Redcliffe itself. Look out for stone markers dotted along the route with "S M R Pipe" written on them. The tradition of the pipe walk began as a way to ensure the route of the pipe had not been compromised by any faults over the preceding year.

296

Bristol steam locomotives are still pulling trains

Bristol was home to two prominent manufacturers of steam locomotives, the Avonside Engine Company (St Phillips) and Peckett and Sons (St George and Fishponds). Some of their engines survived the end of steam and can be found working on preservation lines in New Zealand, Australia, South Africa, and Belgium. Perhaps the most remarkable of these is *Karlskoga*. Built in 1873, it was the first train to operate on (what is now) the Nora Bergslags Veteran Railway (Sweden) and still works to this day. Several, including Peckett's last steam engine, are in the hands of the Sandstone Heritage Trust in South Africa and one is in a former workshop in Bolivia.

297

The "Moulin Rouge" was Bristol's first gay club

The "Moulie" as it came to be known, was re-opened as Bristol's first gay club in October 1970 on Worrall Road, Clifton where an old swimming pool was boarded over to provide for the Moulie's dance floor. OutStories Bristol says the site had been a sports club, bingo hall, a strip club called Lester's, and a dance hall. Dave Prowse, the Bristolian weight-lifting champion who would play the physical role of Darth Vader in the *Star Wars* franchise, was one of the bouncers for a time. As one of the largest gay clubs in the country, the Moulie attracted a broad clientele but started losing out to competition from new venues in the City Centre from the mid-70s.

298

The Bristol Gulls were the first crew to row across the Atlantic in an eco-boat

Lorna Carter, Sofia Deambrosi, and Sarah Hunt Phoebe Wright took part in the 2020 Talisker Whisky Challenge in a boat made of 10,000 recycled bottles. The Talisker Whisky Challenge is widely acknowledged to be the toughest rowing race in the world and the boat was the first of the Atlantic rowing boats to be produced in an environmentally friendly way. The all-female four-boat was named after the critically endangered Vaquita porpoise and raised funds for Clean Up Bristol Harbour and RNLI Portishead. The skipper, Sofia, was the first Uruguay national to row across an ocean.

299

The Commercial Rooms was a private member's club

Established as a meeting place for the city's merchants, the Commercial Rooms' first President was John McAdam, of Macadamisation/Tarmac fame. In a smart little history compiled by A G Powell, he details some of the club's intriguing features which at one time included a weathervane that indicated whether it was safe for ships to leave the City Docks. In the 1950s a tape machine fed stock market information to "The Great Room" and provided the cricket scores during the summer months. The Commercial Rooms predates the Clifton Club by seven years but has subsequently been outlasted. J D Wetherspoons took over the building in 1995.

300

At Pitch and Pay Lane, visitors pitched and paid to avoid the plague

The name given Pitch and Pay Lane in Stoke Bishop is a remnant of a time when visitors would "pitch and pay" to stay just outside of the city for fear of entering it and ending up with the plague themselves. Believed to follow the route of the Roman "Via Julia" road, the end of Pitch and Pay sits on the old boundary between Bristol and what was the countryside surrounding Westbury-on-Trym. A wooden stile is thought to have been erected there in the 1600s where Westbury villagers could bring their wares for sale and Bristolians could throw their coins back at the villagers.

301

Bristol was voted the UK's kindest city in 2016

In a poll of 19 cities, the Co-op surveyed 4,000 adults on the amount of time they spend doing "good deeds". Bristol came top of the survey, with a notable number of 18-25 year-olds regularly helping out their fellow Bristolians. Belfast came in second and London was the "least kind" at 19. It is one of many accolades Bristol has accumulated in recent years, including "tenth happiest city" (OPP), "most artistic city in the UK" (Premier Inn), "best city to live in Britain" (Sunday Times), "world vegan capital" (Chef's Pencil), "best city for students (Whatuni Students), "most musical city" (Telegraph), and "UK's most inspiring city" (Inspiring Cities Ranking 2016).

302

Bristol Rovers unofficial nickname is "The Gas"

The strange nickname is a legacy of Rovers having been based out of Eastville Stadium, then in the downdraft of Stapleton Road Gasworks. Reflecting some years later, a fan said: "Strange, but in some bizarre additive way I looked forward to filling my lungs with that pungent aroma. Maybe it was associating it with the excitement of attending the game." The club played at Eastville Stadium between 1897 and 1986, when financial trouble forced them to move. Officially nicknamed "The Pirates", the use of the term "Gasheads" was originally a taunt used by City fans but has subsequently developed into the club's unofficial nickname.

303

The Bristol Corporation built a hotel at Portishead

The Bristol Corporation was the predecessor to today's City Council and in 1830, it became the only public authority in the UK to fund the construction of a hotel during the 19th century. The aim was to develop Portishead as a tourist destination for the people of Bristol, along similar lines to later developments at Severn Beach. The Corporation funded both the construction of the hotel (now the Grade II listed Royal Inn) and a landing platform on Royal Beach that was subsequently demolished. Fifty years later, the Bristol Corporation purchased Portishead docks and managed the port right up until its closure as an industrial dock in 1992.

304

Wills' Wild Woodbines were a cultural phenomenon

Known as "gaspers" within the industry due to the high tar content of the original unfiltered variety, the Woodbines were an immensely popular cigarette during the first half of the 20th century in large part due to them being cheaper than most of the competitors. Originally launched in 1888, the Woodbines would find themselves in use during WWI, where a chaplain who came to be known as "Woodbine Willie" handed them out on the Western Front. During the 1960s, an attempt to repackage the distinctive Woodbines with plainer white packaging resulted in uproar from their customers.

305

There are remains of a Roman road on the Downs

The Romans are understood to have been the first to build a settlement at what is now Sea Mills, establishing a port called Portus Abonae. The Roman road crossing part of Durdham Down was part of the Via Julia and would have connected the port with Bath (then known as Aquae Sulis) and London (Londinium), long before Bristol came into existence. Portus Abonae provided the crossing to the Roman fortress of Caerleon in Wales. The Via Julia still exists on the Downs as a 100m long hump that runs almost adjacent to Stoke Road on the south side. A section of the road is believed to still be in use in Sneyd Park (now Pitch and Pay Lane and Mariners Path).

306

Bishopston is named after Dr James Monk

The area now known as Bishopston was previously part of the Manor of Horfield, an area of working farmland gifted by the Crown to the city's Augustinian monks and then during the dissolution of the monasteries. In common with much of the Victorian green belt in the mid to late 1800s, Horfield Great Farm (as it was then known) was seen as ripe for development. It was James Monk (Bishop of Gloucester and Bristol) who orchestrated the land sale. Bishopston's Monk Road is named after him, as is Monk Park in Southmead, and several other streets name check the area's history and the people who influenced it.

307

There are two Cabot Towers

There is another Cabot Tower at St John's in the Canadian province of Newfoundland and Labrador. Like the Bristol tower, it was built to commemorate the 400th anniversary of John Cabot's voyage to Newfoundland but also Queen Victoria's Diamond Jubilee. The tower was constructed on the highest point of Signal Hill, arguably better known as the site where the first transatlantic wireless transmission was received (by Marconi in 1901). A wireless station in the tower later sent out one of the first wireless transmissions of the human voice, and today the tower honours Cabot's voyage and the history of wireless communication through an exhibition on Marconi.

308

Clevedon Pier collapsed during stress testing

The load testing of the pier using tanks filled with water was a requirement for insurance purposes. On 16th October 1974, a section of the pier collapsed during load testing leaving the pagoda end of the pier standing by itself. Five years later, Woodspring District Council voted to demolish the remaining pier, provoking national opposition. It was in the blowback against this decision that Sir John Betjeman made his famous remarks about the pier, describing it as "the most beautiful pier in England". As the rest of the structure required work, the subsequent restoration happened in phases with a grand reopening taking place in 1998. In 2001, the pier was given Grade I listed status.

309

The oldest operating steam vessel in Britain was built in Bristol

"Bertha" is a drag boat believed to have been built by Lunnel, G & Co of Bristol in 1844. Her role was to clear mud from the floor of Bridgewater's harbour, not by dredging but by shifting mud (dragging) using a rectangular sheet of metal hung beneath the hull. The mud was pushed to a position where the outgoing tide would take it out into the Severn Estuary. She continued to work the Port of Bridgewater right up until 1968 after which she became a museum ship at various destinations, and was designated as one of the 200 vessels in the National Historic Fleet.

310

A Bristol Britannia aircraft crashed in Downend

On 6th November 1957, a prototype commercial airliner built in Bristol crashed near Overndale Road, Downend. All 15 crew members died in the incident, the cause of which has never been officially established. The area where the crash took place has since been named Britannia Wood and a plaque honouring the men who lost their lives has been placed on the Downend Folk House. Like the Brabazon, the Britannia was a jet-prop plane (the first to operate at long range) in an increasingly jet-powered world. Only 85 were ever built but the "Whispering Giant" proved popular with operators and one is still in existence at Cotswold Airport.

311

The 1801 *Bristol Packet* is a scheduled ancient monument

Due to its ongoing importance as a major shipping route, many wrecks in the River Severn have been cleared using explosives, including one that required 117 tonnes to remove it. The wreck believed to be that of the *Bristol Packet* (built 1801) is now a protected site at Madbrain Sands, Minehead. Built in New England, it had a service life of just seven years and now makes an appearance only when severe weather exposes the "bones" of the vessel, which are usually fully covered. Above ground, there are seven Bristol-built ships beached further up the Severn at Purton Hulks (Britain's largest ship graveyard) near Gloucester.

312

Portishead is named after Portishead

Portishead (North Somerset) gets its name from having been at the "head" of the River Avon which is now obscured from view by Royal Portbury Dock. Portishead (the band) formed in Bristol in 1991 and are regularly referred to as pioneers of the trip-hop genre. Their debut album garnered critical acclaim and secured both a Mercury Prize for Best Album and Edison Award for Best International Dance/Rap. They've come to lament what's happened to Bristol in the intervening years, complaining that gentrification ruined those parts of the city that had done so much to influence their sound. Geoff Barrow, the band's instrumentalist, isn't too fond of Portishead (the town) either.

313

Princess Eleanor of Brittany was the longest imprisoned member of an English royal family

Eleanor was heir to the Duchy of Brittany and a significant area of land in both England and France (Anjou, Aquitaine, and Brittany). This, and the potential that she would bear a male heir if she was allowed to have children, meant that both her uncle King John and King Henry III had her imprisoned from 1204 until her death in 1241. She may have also spent time at Corfe Castle as well as Bristol Castle during this period but sources vary on her exact whereabouts. She died at Bristol Castle and for a while was buried at St James's Priory.

314

The second largest ship in the world wrecked in the Avon

Surpassed in size only by the SS Great Britain, the SS Demerara was built for the West India Mail Steamship Company in 1851. On 10th November of that year, she was towed out of the Cumberland Basin en route to have her engines fitted. The tide had already started falling and the pilot of the tug tried to make up for lost time by increasing speed. This resulted in the ship running aground and then getting caught by the falling tide. Wedged between the two banks of the Avon and heavily damaged, the ship was eventually towed out, sold and renamed "The British Empire".

315

Cabot's Circus was nearly called Merchants' Quarter

Back in 2006, the original plan for the retail district was to call it Merchants' Quarter. However, many felt the name was too evocative of Bristol's imperial history and in particular its role in the slave trade. John Cabot, whose voyage to Newfoundland was one of the most significant journeys in the lead up to European colonisation of the New World, was given the namesake instead. In his home country, a university in Rome established in the 1970s was named in his honour and given the motto *explorando excello*. The explorer has a number of sites in Canada named after him including two schools, several roads, an Italian members club, parkland, and a parkland trail.

316

Lady Apsley was Bristol's first female MP

Violet Emily Mildred Meeking married Allen Algernon Bathurst (Lord Apsley) in 1924. The heir to the 15,000 acre Bathurst Estate, Lord Apsley served in WWI and later became MP for Southampton and then Bristol Central. Lord Aplsey was killed in an air crash in 1942, and his seat was contested and won by Lady Apsley. A horse riding accident in 1930 had left Lady Aplsey without the use of her legs and she gave her maiden speech in the House of Commons from her wheelchair. She was MP for Bristol Central 1943-45, losing out when the national landslide removed Churchill from power. Both the Bathurst Earldom and the Bathurst Estate have survived.

317

Elsie Griffin was born here

A blue plaque on the side of St Michael on the Mount Primary School commemorates the life of one of the most influential singers of the early 20th century. Elsie Griffin was born on St Michael's Hill in 1895 and went on to work as a chocolate packer for Fry's. She was recognised locally as a musical child prodigy and made her professional break into music singing songs to the troops throughout WWI. It was during the war that Griffin popularised both "Danny Boy" (the pipes, the pipes are calling) and the "Roses of Picardy", two of the era's best-known songs. After the war, Griffin was principal soprano in the D'Oyly Carte opera company, cementing her reputation as one of leading sopranos of the inter-war period.

318

Bristol was the first city in the Europe to declare a climate emergency

On 13th November 2018, a motion proposed by Green Party councillor Carla Denyer was passed unanimously at Bristol City Council. It committed the city to achieve carbon neutral status by 2030, a full 20 years earlier than the previous commitment. In the subsequent years, over 300 councils chose to declare climate emergencies, along with the Welsh Assembly, London Assembly, UK Parliament, and Scottish Government. Bristol became the first city in the UK to declare an ecological emergency in 2020.

319

Churchill was attacked by a Suffragette at Temple Meads

Winston Churchill arrived in Bristol on 15th November, 1909, ahead of the Anchor Society's 140th anniversary dinner at Colston Hall that evening. Then Home Secretary for the Liberal Party, Churchill was approached at the station by Theresa Garnett who wielded a dog whip and is said to have shouted "Take that in the name of the insulted women of England". Churchill sustained a minor injury to his face and did not appear in court to press charges. Garnett was sent to HM Prison Bristol (Horfield) for disturbing the peace. Churchill later voted against votes for women.

320

Failure to pass the Second Reform Bill led to Bristol's biggest riot

The Second Reform Bill of 1831 aimed to do away with the infamous "rotten boroughs" and broaden electoral representation in Britain's growing industrial cities. When the House of Lords voted down the Bill, the rioting that followed resulted in (possibly) hundreds of deaths and the destruction of property. The palace of the Bishop of Bristol, the home of the Lord Mayor of Bristol, and the New Gaol (now Abel Yard/Hope Quay) were all attacked and burnt. A new bill was put forward and became the Great Reform Act of 1832.

321

Bristol's 2019 population was estimated to be 468,400

Although Bristol's time as the country's "second city" is well behind it, the city is comfortably the largest in the South West and one of Britain's 10 "core cities". In common with many British cities, Bristol experienced a sizable growth in population in the 19th century, from 59,526 in 1801 (more than double the estimated population in 1700) to 297,932 in 1891. It peaked in the mid 20th century before dropping off and then rising again in the 2000s. Bristol's population (counting the unitary authority area only) rose considerably in the ten years up to 2018, with 44,400 people moving to the city, more than the national average growth of a UK city.

322

Damien Hirst was born in Bristol

Banksy has become synonymous with Bristol thanks to the street art dotted around the city but he is not the only globally famous artist. Damien Hirst was born in Bristol in 1965 and became well-known for his *Natural History* series which features dead animals in formaldehyde. In 2008, Hirst secured the biggest sales for a one-artist auction, raising £111m at Sotheby's. At this point he was widely reported to be the UK's richest living artist. During the Covid-19 crisis Hirst donated the original *Butterfly Rainbow* (which had raised £1,508,172 for NHS Charities Together through prints) to University Hospitals Bristol and Weston NHS Foundation Trust (UHBW).

323

The Bristol Jamia Mosque in Totterdown was the first mosque in the city

Boasting capacity for 840 people, the largest mosque in the South West was also the city's first. The building originally housed a Holy Nativity Church missionary and was known as St Katherine's Church. The Bristol Muslim Association rented the church and later purchased it for £2,500 in the 1970s. In 1979, the building was significantly altered to include a dome and a non-functioning 88-metre-high minaret. In 2016, the mosque made national news when a small group of racists were said to have thrown bacon sandwiches at it.

324

The last floating wooden lightship in the world is berthed in Bathurst Basin

Originally commissioned by Trinity House as Light Vessel 55 and subsequently renamed the John Sebastian, the lightship's original purpose was to warn sailors off the shifting sandbanks of the River Severn. She was built by Charles Hill & Sons in the Albion Yard in 1885 and went into service a year later. LV55 was in service right up until 1954 when her parts were sold off and her two sister ships were scrapped. It was expected that LV55 would also be scrapped but the vessel was saved by a group of enthusiasts and is now preserved as a clubhouse for the Cabot Cruising Club.

325

Mary Wollstonecraft wrote her only complete novel in Bristol

Best known as the author of *A Vindication of the Rights of Woman* and a leading feminist of her age, Mary Wollstonecraft is less well known as the author of *Mary: A Fiction*, her only complete novel. She wrote the book whilst working as a governess for Lord and Lady Kingsborough on Sion Hill in Clifton. Mary borrowed extensively from her experiences as a governess and is said to have based the character of Eliza on Lady Kingsborough. Another novel, *The Cave of Fancy*, was begun in Bristol, but never completed.

326

Eleven People died in the Bristol Bridge Riot

There has been a Bristol Bridge near today's Castle Park since Saxon times with the first stone structure appearing in the 1200s. In 1794, opposition grew against the renewal of tolls on the bridge, the construction of which had been funded partly with public money. 11 people died and a further 45 people were injured in the ensuing conflict which had gone down as one of the biggest civil disturbances in the UK during the 18th century.

327

American First Lady Eleanor Roosevelt visited Bristol in November 1941

The wife of the then US President had a packed itinerary when she visited the city in November 1942. Her visit included a tour of war-damaged Bristol where she was given a naval guard of honour with officers displaying a Nazi flag captured at Dieppe. She then dropped in to the two segregated "white" and "coloured" American Red Cross clubs, viewed the Wills Hall rest centre, enjoyed a sherry with the Lord Mayor at Council House and was shown an "exhibition of part-time women war workers".

328

Castle Park was once a shopping district

In the first of six high intensity bombing runs on the city, on the night of 24th November 1940, 148 bombers of the Luftflotte 3 division unloaded around 12,000 incendiary devices and 160 tonnes of explosives onto central Bristol. The campaign lasted over six hours and focused on what is now Castle Park. 204 people lost their lives in the inferno that followed. Now a council-owned park, the area had been a busy medieval commercial quarter, in the shadows of the Norman Bristol Castle. What little remained of the district was demolished in the 1960s. Two ruined churches (St Mary Le Port and St Peter's) and the cellars of the bombed-out houses and shops are all that is left.

329

There have been four railway stations in the Gorge

The Hotwells end of the underground line that ran to Clifton is still visible from Portway as the Clifton Rocks Railway station. But there was once another station here called the Hotwells Halt which was constructed during WWI to help transport workers down to Avonmouth. It was part of the Bristol Port and Pier line, which ran alongside the Avon Gorge to the east. An earlier Hotwells Railway Station was opened on the Port and Pier line in 1865 and closed in 1922 during the construction of Portway. On the west side of the gorge, the Nightingale Valley Halt was part of the Portishead Railway and operated by GWR between 1928 and 1932.

330

Bristol produced the world's first tandem-rotor twin engine helicopter

Only three Type 173s were built but they laid the groundwork for the development of the 192 Belvedere, which was commissioned and used by the RAF. To date, the Belvedere is the only British tandem-rotor twin engine helicopter to enter production and saw action in the Middle East and Borneo. The concept of a helicopter with two engines and two rotors is best represented by Boeing's CH-47 Chinook. This was developed after the Bristol variations but has served a longer operational life most notably with the US military.

331

Jane Couch made female boxing legal in the UK

Jane moved to Bristol from Lancashire aged 25 and became a world-famous boxer, securing six world championship wins. Having discovered a natural talent for boxing at her local gym, Jane soon discovered that female boxing was still illegal in the UK, even in the 1990s. She initially took the case for legalisation to the British Board of Boxing Control who told her that they would not change the rules in part because they believed women would be too "unstable" to fight. Jane took her case to the High Court on the grounds of sexual discrimination and restriction of trade and fought the first legalised women's boxing match in the UK in 1998.

332

Michael Dillon was the first person to undergo gender reassignment surgery

Born to an aristocratic Irish family as Laura Dillon in 1915, Michael Dillon moved to Bristol in 1939. He worked in a garage, by which point he had adopted a male identity and was referred to by the other garage staff as a man. He began both his hormonal and surgical transition while in Bristol during the 1940s, during which time he also served as a fire watcher – looking out for incendiary devices during the Bristol Blitz. After the news of his transition became public in the 1950s, Michael moved to India and lived briefly in a Buddhist monastery before his death in 1962.

333

Tony Benn was a local MP

Benn took his seat as MP for Bristol South East on 30th November 1950. A by-election had been held due to the declining health of the former MP, Sir Stafford Cripps CH QC, a major figure in the Labour Party who had been Chancellor of the Exchequer up to that point. Benn temporarily lost the seat in 1961 when he inherited a peerage from his father who had been Viscount Stansgate and the Tories challenged the 1961 election result. He retook the seat from the Conservatives in 1963, when the Peerage Act allowed Benn to renounce his peerage. Benn was one of the most prominent Labour politicians of his day and a vocal supporter of the continuation of the Concorde project at Filton, which was constantly threatened with cancellation due to cost overruns.

334

The first St Pauls Carnival was held in 1968

Not long after the end of WWII, people from Britain's overseas territories made their way to Bristol to make a new life for themselves and fill the UK's post-war skills gap. St Pauls proved to be a popular destination for people from Asia, Ireland, and the Caribbean as the still bomb-damaged area was known to have relatively cheap housing stock. The city's longest running street festival began as a way to bind these different communities together, celebrate the community's cultures, and present a positive image of the St Pauls area. In the subsequent decades, the carnival has grown in scope and continued to be a firm Bristol fixture. It celebrated its 50th year in 2018.

335

50 million litres of water are pumped out of the Severn Tunnel every day

The Severn Tunnel was the longest underwater tunnel in the world until 1987 and the longest mainline railway tunnel in the UK until new tunnels were built for HS1 in 2007. Designed by Sir John Hawkshaw, who with William Barlow was responsible for completing the Clifton Suspension Bridge, drainage problems began with the excavation of "the Great Spring" in 1879, necessitating the use of continuous pumping which still takes place today. The first passenger trains crossed the tunnel on 1st December 1886, 14 years after the project to build the tunnel began.

336

Three *SS Bristol City* ships were lost at sea

The Bristol City Line operated a cargo service between Bristol, New York and Montreal. The first *SS Bristol City* went missing somewhere between New York and Bristol in December 1880. The second was torpedoed by the German U-Boat U.94 during WWI with the loss of 30 lives and the third was torpedoed by U.358 during WWII. Another Bristol City Line ship, *SS Bath City* sank off the Grand Banks having sprung a leak in 1881 and the second was wrecked on Lundy Island in the Bristol Channel in 1900. The first and only ship to be named *SS Coombe Dingle* ran aground and sank off Carnalea, Bangor, while the first of three *SS Wells City* ships collided with another vessel and sank but was later recovered by another firm.

337

A pioneer of trip hop was born in Knowle West

Adrian Thaws was born in 1968 to a Jamaican father and Anglo-Guyanese mother in Knowle West. Now known by his stage name Tricky, his mother died when he was just four years old and Left in the care of his grandmother, Tricky was involved in gangs and crime from an early age but still managed to carve out a successful career as a rapper and record producer. He went on to be one of the original members of the Bristol-originated Massive Attack band before going solo in 1995. His seventh studio album, released in 2008, was called *Knowle West Boy* and was a nod to his challenging childhood and teenage years.

338

Otters and kingfishers have been found in Eastville Park

In the late 19th century, a movement to establish public parkland for working people started to gain traction amongst Victorian do-gooders, keen to alleviate the conditions created by industrialisation and rapid population growth. In Bristol, this resulted in the purchase of several sites that were developed into publicly owned and free-to-enter parkland. Covering a total of 70 acres, Eastville Park was the largest of these, and was bought off Ashton Court's Sir Greville Smyth for £30,878 in 1889. It has become a hotspot for local wildlife, including Otters which have been found across Bristol's 100 miles of waterways, and their numbers appear to be on the increase.

339

Troopers Hill may not be named after Troopers

Now a 21-acre council-owned nature reserve, Troopers Hill (St George) has passed through the hands of several owners as well as being a site for several intensive industries over the last few centuries. The land had once been owned by the Truebody family and was known as Truebody's Hill as late as the 19th century when the Ordnance Survey formalised the use of the word "Troopers". In 1645, parliamentary forces fighting in the English Civil War camped on the hill prior to the Second Siege of Bristol. It is likely that Troopers is both a corruption of Truebody and a nod to the area's Civil War history.

340

Bristol was hit by two IRA bombs in December 1974

Just after 8pm on 18th December 1974, Park Street was hit by two IRA bombs. The IRA had notified the police to expect the first of these bombs, which blew up outside a Dixon's shop. The second bomb had been placed inside a dustbin and exploded nine minutes later outside the Kenneth Harris hearing aid shop. The warning of the first explosion meant the police were able to largely clear Park Street and only 20 people were injured. The Provisional IRA returned in December 1978, detonating another bomb that injured seven people in Clifton while a second bomb was found at Swan National Car Rental on Fairfax Street.

341

Bristol is a UNESCO City of Film

There are 18 Cities of Film dotted around the world, each committed to "delivering meaningful and progressive programmes of work that contribute to sustainable urban development". The designation is a permanent recognition of Bristol's long standing reputation as a world leader in the film production which began with William Friese-Green's innovations in moving images back in the 19th century. Born in Bristol in 1855, Friese-Green was a pioneer of film production, noted for his motion picture cameras that recorded film footage as early as 1889. Other Cities of Film include Bradford, Rome, Qingdao, Sarajevo, and Wellington.

342

The official opening of the Clifton Suspension Bridge featured a 21-gun salute

Plagued with financial trouble, it took 33 years to finish the bridge, by which point Isambard Kingdom Brunel had passed away. The official opening took place on 8th December 1864, and was a day of considerable ceremony, featuring traders from the Old City processing up to the bridge, a military procession, 16 marching bands, a light display, and 150,000 spectators. The day after, the bridge opened to the public. 21-year-old Mary Griffiths raced a boy across the bridge, beating him by just a few metres to become the first person to cross the new bridge.

343

A Bristol cotton factory was the largest outside of the North-West

The enormous Great Western Cotton Factory relied on the labour of around 900 women and children when it opened in 1839. According to Dr Mike Richardson: "Barton Hill workers endured long working hours, wage reductions, high rates of industrial accidents and ill-health from the cotton dust and humidity". Richardson has revealed records of worker resistance against their conditions as well as the extent to which compensation pay-outs to slave owners provided the funds to start the firm. The factory finally closed in 1925 and most of the remaining buildings were demolished in 1968.

344

Hannah Penn was the first woman to be made an Honorary Citizen of the US

As of 2021, there have only been eight Honorary Citizens of the United States. Hannah is one, and her husband William Penn is another. Hannah was born in Bristol in 1671 and married William Penn 1696. When William Penn was unable to act as Governor of Pennsylvania due to ill-health, Hannah effectively took on the position and continued to do so for eight years after his death. Ronald Reagan bestowed honorary citizen status by Act of Congress in 1984, and in 2013, the state of Pennsylvania had its first annual Hannah Callowhill Penn Day.

345

Bristol engines powered the nation's nuclear deterrent

The Avro Vulcan "V bomber" was a high-altitude bomber aircraft and the largest delta winged aircraft ever produced. The Vulcan went into service in 1956, powered by engines developed by three successive Bristol-based firms, the Bristol Aerospace Company, Bristol Siddeley and Rolls-Royce. 26 dispersal sites were established to ensure the deterrent could be maintained in the event of an attack on the Vulcan's main bases. RAF Filton was selected as one of those bases. The Vulcan was the first aircraft to carry Britain's nuclear weapons and provided the nation's nuclear deterrent right up until the Royal Navy's submarines took on the Polaris missiles in 1970.

346

Bristol is name-checked in Van Morrison's "Summertime in England"

Almost 16 minutes long, "Summertime in England" is the Northern Irish singer's longest song in the "Cry Me Home" album. Van the Man has been a regular at the Colston Hall (now Bristol Beacon) and has also performed at the Hippodrome. In another song, "Cleaning Windows", Van Morrison buys a packet of Will's Woodbines.

Won't you meet me down Bristol
Meet me along by Bristol
We'll go ridin' down
Down by Avalon

347

Churchill was Chancellor of the University of Bristol

Churchill was installed as Chancellor on 13th December 1929 and held the position right up until his death in 1965. This has so-far made him the university's longest standing Chancellor. On the day he took up the role, students carried him from the Wills Memorial Building to the Victoria Rooms, where he took part in the university's "RAG" society play, which saw him tried and arrested. Churchill returned to the university in 1941 to confer honorary degrees on the US ambassador and the Prime Minister of Australia. The night before, the Great Hall had been destroyed in a German bombing raid but Churchill insisted the ceremony take place in the nearby Reception Room.

348

Prince Philip donated *The Matthew's* mast

The Duke's interest in maritime history made him an important partner in the effort to rescue the SS Great Britain in the 70s. In the 1990s, with the anniversary of Cabot's voyage to the New World approaching, Prince Philip became a patron of the organisation set up to build the replica caravel and donated the ship's main mast. He also "laid the keel" of the ship, traditionally the moment when the start of construction is formally recognised. The Duke steered *The Matthew* for most of her journey out of Bristol docks on 2nd May 1997 and flew out to Cape Bonavista with Queen Elizabeth to receive the ship at the end of its voyage.

349

The Bristol Lido was the country's first electrically heated swimming pool

Originally built as the Clifton Victoria Baths, the Bristol Lido opened to much acclaim in July 1850. Like the then-incomplete Suspension Bridge, the new baths showed off Ancient Egyptian design cues, and quickly became an important social hub. Electric heating was installed in the 1930s and the pool remained in operation until 1990, with a major leak cited as the main reason for closure. A successful application for Grade II listed status in 1998 meant the Lido was spared the wrecking ball and it was reopened by the Glass Boat Company in 2008.

350

Bristol Zoo is mentioned in a Goldie Lookin Chain song

The 2004 track by the Newport-based group reached No.3 in the UK Singles Chart, whilst the album *Greatest Hits* got to No.5 in the UK Album Chart. The song parodied the American hip hop culture of the early 2000s and although the band had five other charted singles, *Guns Don't Kill People* proved to be their biggest chart success.

Guns don't kill people rappers do,
From Bristol Zoo to B&Q,
I want to rap, I want to rhyme
Heard it in a song now I'm into gun crime,

351

The Bristol Stool Chart classifies poo into seven categories

Developed by the Bristol Royal Infirmary in 1997, the chart has gone on to be used as an aid to bowel research worldwide. The categories are as follows:
Type 1: Separate hard lumps, like nuts
Type 2: Sausage-shaped, but lumpy
Type 3: Like a sausage but with cracks on its surface
Type 4: Like a sausage or snake, smooth and soft
Type 5: Soft blobs with clear cut edges
Type 6: Fluffy pieces with ragged edges, a mushy stool
Type 7: Watery, no solid pieces, entirely liquid

352

WWI U-Boats were brought into Bristol City Docks

Surely one of the strangest historic photos of Bristol is the sight of two WWI German U-Boats being towed into the City Centre and exhibited to the public in December 1918. One of the two boats was U.86, which had torpedoed and sunk the hospital ship *Llandovery Castle*, just six months earlier. Clearly marked as a hospital ship, its sinking was against the rules of war. 234 people died, including around 90 Bristolians. As Eugene Byrne notes in his account of this episode, none of the Bristolians who gathered to see the two ships moored outside the Hippodrome knew the submarine had been involved in this infamous war crime.

353

Mary Perkins, co-founder of Specsavers, was born here

Dame Mary Perkins DBE was born in her grandmother's house on St Michael's Hill in 1944. She later moved to Sea Mills, and then to a council estate in Henbury. She met her Welsh husband Doug Perkins in 1962 and the couple set up a chain of opticians in Bristol which was sold for £2 million in 1980. Shortly after that, Mary's parents retired on the island of Guernsey, and the couple made the decision to join them. It was there that they founded Specsavers and forever changed the way high street opticians operate. Specsavers went on to become the world's largest private opticians, making Mary one of the UK's few billionaires.

354

Averys were the first UK wine merchants to import New Zealand wines

Established in 1793, Averys became the first UK wine merchant to import commercial Australian wine in 1966, bringing Penfolds Grange into the country for the first time. Five years earlier, the company's historic cellars had been the training ground for the Australian winemaker Wolf Bass, who learnt to blend wines under the tutelage of Ronald Avery. In 1978, Ronald's son, John imported the first commercial New Zealand wines to the UK and is credited with having introduced many New World wines to the UK, as well as changing perceptions towards wines from those markets.

355

The Antarctic Bamber Glacier is named after a Bristol professor

In 2020, the British Antarctic Territory designated several new place names to commemorate the 200th anniversary of the discovery of Antarctica. As a leading polar scientist, Jonathan Bamber, Professor of Physical Geography, was chosen in recognition of his contribution to our understanding of the frozen continent. At the time of the designation, the Bamber Glacier was 9km long and 2km wide. Another place name was given to a 950-metre Antarctic mountain which is now known as the Dobson Dome after Bristol-educated civil servant Alan Dobson.

356

Guild Heritage House was one of the first accessible buildings in the country

Now converted to flats, the building was funded by an organisation known as the Guild of the Brave Poor Things and aimed to provide a place of respite and development for isolated disabled people in the city. The House on Braggs Lane, Old Market, was built in 1913 by architect Sir Frank Wills, who also designed the City Museum. Boasting a wide entrance and completely level first floor, it is thought to be the first accessible building in the country and included space for performances, lectures and craft apprenticeships.

357

Queen's Hall on Peter Street was the city's first purpose-built cinema

Early cinemas were generally conversions of pre-existing theatre spaces. Queen's Hall, built in the Old City in 1910, was the first Bristol building designed to be a cinema but its most memorable characteristic was arguably the partially retractable roof, installed so that the staff could vent cigarette smoke. It was replaced with the News Theatre Cinema, a radically different architectural proposition: a monolithic block with an art-deco interior. It opened on 22nd December, 1933. Unlike most of Peter Street, the News Theatre survived the war and closed in 1956.

358

Agatha Christie got married in Clifton

It was Christmas Eve 1914 and the 24-year-old Agatha Mary Clarissa Miller did not have time to find wedding clothes. She had decided to marry her partner just the day before and was determined to make best use of Captain Archibald Christie's brief respite from the Royal Flying Corp. Archibald had been a student at Clifton College, where his stepfather was a teacher and nearby Emmanuel Church was chosen as the venue. Archibald rose to the rank of Colonel during WWI. Agatha went on to sell two billion books. They were divorced in 1926 and Emmanuel Church was later converted to flats.

359

Christmas Steps gets its name from knife smiths.

The street was not always called Christmas Steps, having been named after Queen Elizabeth (Queene Street) following her visit to the city in 1574. No one is completely certain as to how the street got its name but like many historic place names, Christmas Steps is probably the corruption of an earlier word, in this case *Knyfesmyth* – Middle English for knife-smith. Knife-smiths were once present near Christmas Steps, on a road known as *Knyfesmyth Street.* An alternative theory put forward for the name of the street comes from its proximity to the Chapel of the Three Kings of Cologne which features statues of the Three Wise Men and a nativity scene in the church window.

360

Sarah Anne Bright produced the earliest photographs by a woman

Sarah Anne, who is related to both the Gibbs and Bright families of Bristol, was recently discovered to be the woman behind the Quillan Leaf, a photogram taken in 1839. Amazingly, this fact was only determined in 2015, when an album found its way to Sotheby's in New York and required closer inspection before listing. Larry Schaaf was able to identify Sarah's initials on the print. The Bright family were major beneficiaries of plantation ownership and slavery in the Caribbean, as well as banking and business interests in the city, they once owned part of a firm that operated the SS Great Britain.

361

Europe's largest tobacco plant was in Hartcliffe

The enormous Imperial Tobacco site opened in 1974 and precipitated the closure of the factories in Bedminster and Ashton. It was a state-of-the-art plant in its day and had been intended to produce cigarettes for a still-flourishing market both in the UK and abroad. But the Hartcliffe plant lasted just 16 years with production moving to Nottingham. Imperial Tobacco continued to operate in the city and the site of the former factory became Imperial Park. The closure of the factory, and the resulting unemployment, had huge consequences for thc Hartcliffe area.

362

72,000 Bristol residents were suffering from income deprivation in 2018

Bristol City Council's Health and Wellbeing report for 2018 also found that Bristol's highest earners were making six times more than the city's poorest. The top 10 percent were found to be earning £899 per week on average in 2017, compared with £154 per week for the bottom ten per cent. Around 16 percent of Bristol's population were living in the "10 percent most deprived areas in England" in 2015, with Hartcliffe, Filwood, and Lawrence Hill reporting the greatest levels of deprivation. The 72,000 income deprived residents made up 17 percent of Bristol's population in 2018.

363

No Snuff at Snuff Mills

Snuff Mills is often thought to have been a site for producing snuff, the popular smokeless tobacco product made from ground tobacco leaves. The name instead originates from the fondness for snuff exhibited by one of the area's millers, "Snuffy Jack", who is said to have turned up to work covered in snuff. It has been suggested that Jack did in fact work for a snuff mill further up the River Frome, known as Witherly's, which at one time was operated by Wills. Purchased by the Corporation in 1926, Snuff Mills is now one of Bristol's most memorable walking destinations and features a restored corn mill near the entrance.

364

Bedminster had its very own Hippodrome

Designed by Bertie Crewe in 1911 for the Variety theatre chain, the Bedminster Hippodrome on East Street was an imposing building that could seat up to 3,000 people. In 1915, it was converted for use as a cinema hall and was renamed the Bedminster Hippodrome Cinema boasting (according to the new owners) “a magnificent orchestral organ, specially built at enormous cost”. On 3rd January 1941, the Hippodrome was hit by Luftwaffe bombs, destroying the roof and much of the auditorium. There was no commercial interest in restoring the building and, shortly after the war ended, Bedminster’s Hippodrome was demolished.

365

Aztec West is a shortening of "A to Z of Technology"

Opened by Margaret Thatcher in December 1989, the business park has become home to over 100 companies mostly notably from the technology sector. The site is less well known for its architecture, some of which has Grade II listed status. Numbers 210, 220, 240, 250, 260, and 290 Park Avenue were designed by Campbell Zogolovitch Wilkinson and Gough and built 1987-88. Historic England describes the buildings as a *"key project by CZWG, a celebrated British Post-Modernist practice[...]a good example of a commercial development in the Post-Modern style, combining bold geometries, polychromy and traditional materials to dynamic effect".*

Know Bristol

About the Author

Ashley Coates is an Anglo-Indian writer and former journalist. Born in Stoke-on-Trent, his family moved to Bristol in 1990. Graduating with First-Class Honours in History in 2012, Ashley completed a Journalism Masters and wrote features for the *Evening Standard* and *Independent* titles. He covered Brexit and environment policy during his time in the UK Parliament and Civil Service.

One Book = One Tree

Every book purchased is funding the planting of a tree through a Bristol-based social enterprise, Ecologi, and the Eden Reforestation Projects. These trees are mostly planted in Madagascar, Nicaragua, Kenya, Uganda and Mozambique. Depending on where you have purchased this book, it is printed on either FSC or FSC Mix paper.

Lightning Source UK Ltd.
Milton Keynes UK
UKHW020125290822
407933UK00008B/682